DISCOVERING
VINTAGE
Las Vegas

DISCOVERING VINTAGE Las Vegas

A Guide to the City's Timeless Shops, Restaurants, Casinos & More

First Edition

PAUL W. PAPA

Guilford, Connecticut
Helena, Montana
An imprint of Rowman & Littlefield

All the information in this guidebook is subject to change. We recommend that you call ahead to obtain current information before traveling.

Globe Pequot is an imprint of Rowman & Littlefield

Distributed by NATIONAL BOOK NETWORK

Copyright © 2014 by Rowman & Littlefield

British Library Cataloguing-in-Publication Information available

Library of Congress Cataloging-in-Publication Data available

ISBN 978-1-4930-0645-8

∞ The paper used in this publication meets the minimum requirements of American National Standard for Information Sciences—Permanence of Paper for Printed Library Materials, ANSI/NISO Z39.48-1992.

Contents

About the Author

Paul W. Papa is a full-time writer who has lived in Las Vegas for more than twenty years (making him vintage as well). He developed a fascination with the town, and all its wonders, while working for close to fifteen years at several Las Vegas casinos. In his role as a security officer, Paul was the person who actually shut and locked the doors of the Sands Hotel and Casino for the final time. He eventually became a hotel investigator for a major Strip casino, during which time he developed a love for writing true stories about uncommon events. He now owns a business that concentrates on nonfiction, technical, and commercial writing. Paul is the author of several books on Las Vegas including *It Happened in Las Vegas: Remarkable Events That Shaped History* and *Haunted Las Vegas: Famous Phantoms, Creepy Casinos, and Gambling Ghosts*. When not at his keyboard, Paul can be found talking to tourists on Freemont Street, investigating some old building, or sitting in a local diner hunting down his next story.

For Norma, who understood the importance of history and held it dear.

Acknowledgments

I would first and foremost like to thank all those people who sat with me and told me their wonderfully intriguing stories. This book is the direct result of people who love what they do and do what they love and I am honored to have been able to capture their stories and pass them on to future generations. I would also like to thank all those people who suggested places to write about. I couldn't have done this book without you all. A special thanks goes out to Karen Green, curator of the National Atomic Testing Museum, for giving me my own personal tour, Laura Hutton at the Boulder Dam Hotel, Mark P. Hall-Patton at the Clark County Museum, and Geoff Schumacher at the Mob Museum. Special thanks also go out to Max Jacobson-Fried who assisted in my research by providing me with some very tasty treats, Evan Glusman who was responsible for one of the best Italian meals my wife and I ever had, Lindsay Wold who gave me some great chocolate, Roger Ghormley who treated my family to Southern-style catfish, Neriza Johnson who showed me why her family is famous for tamales, and Tim Jensen for a couple of scrumptious steaks. Thanks also to my wife, Melissa Papa, who read every story before it was finalized, kept my grammar on track, and made some very valuable suggestions. Finally, I'd like to thank my wonderful editor, Tracee Williams, for her insight, guidance, and obvious desire to make this the best book it could possibly be—thanks!

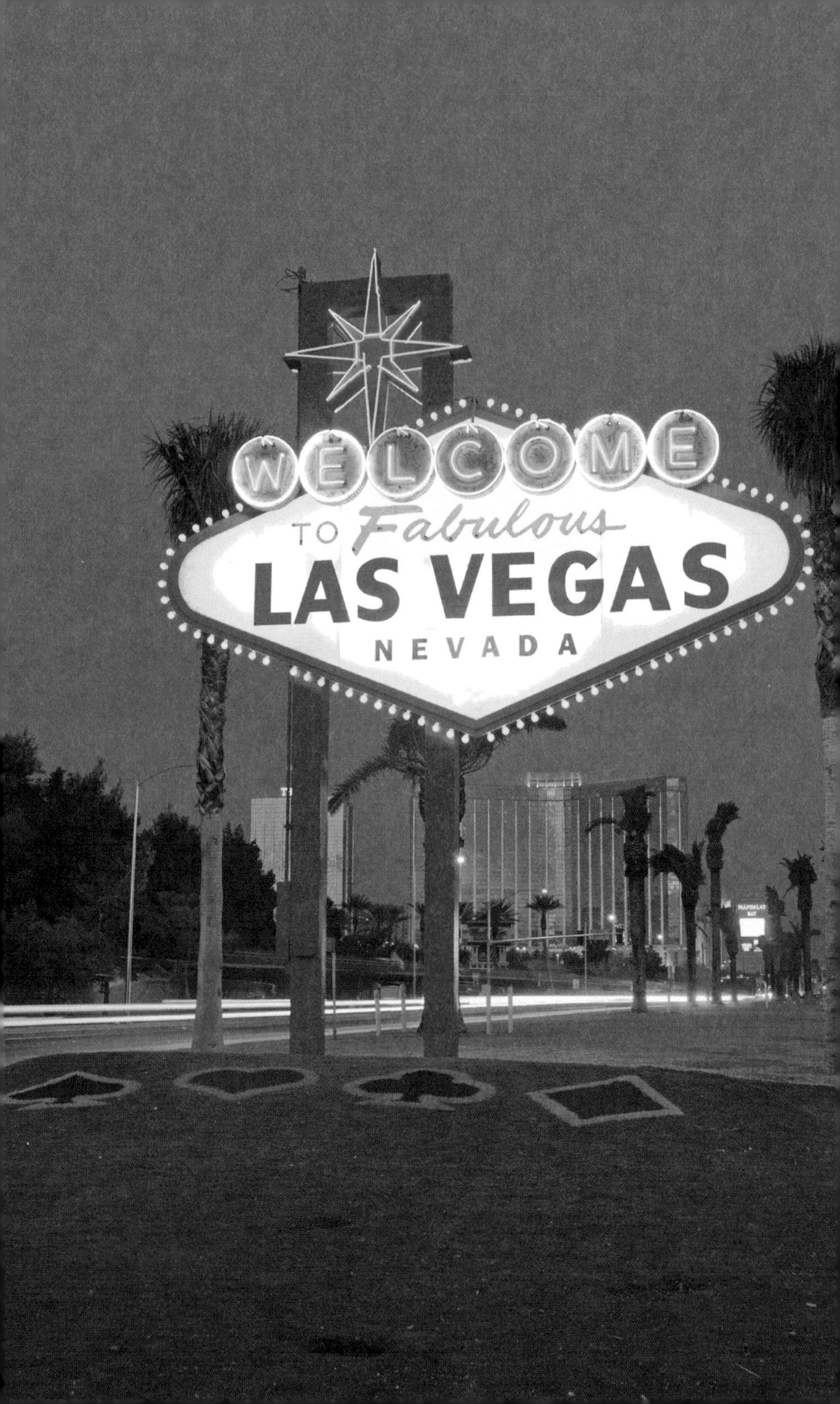
WELCOME
TO Fabulous
LAS VEGAS
NEVADA

Introduction

I live in a beautifully strange town, one that both honors its past and destroys it. As old casinos are imploded to make way for the new, in Las Vegas the term "vintage" can take on a whole new meaning. Add to this the fact that Las Vegas is barely one hundred years old, and you'll quickly discover that finding anything vintage can present quite a challenge. But the valley is full of history—that is, if you know where to look. As Las Vegas progressed from a sleepy little train stop on the way to California to becoming the entertainment capital of the world, many businesses—and casinos—simply ceased to exist. Some, however, withstood the test of time and are still serving the community. And believe it or not, in a city that turns an implosion into a media event, there are some buildings that have lasted since the time when Vegas was still largely made of tents.

Writing a book that deals with old but still existing businesses can pose its own obstacles. Sometimes, despite the best of efforts, the book of history can close on some of those businesses before you get to tell their story. Such was the case with the El Sombrero Café, which, up until a few months ago, had been in operation since 1950, making it the oldest restaurant in Las Vegas. Now that restaurant is no more—and so too is the story I wrote about it. My apologies go to Gary "Whitey" Porteus, his brother Russ "The Patriarch" Porteus, and their friend John Ennesser, loyal patrons of El Sombrero Café who were excited about being in the book. Hopefully they'll find another place to make the loser wear that sombrero.

The problem with writing a book about vintage places is deciding how to define the term vintage. Certainly vintage means old, but a book about "old" places in Las Vegas just didn't seem fitting. So, as writers are prone to do, I turned to my well-worn dictionary and found a definition that seemed to suit my needs. "Vintage: Of old, recognized, and enduring interest, importance, or quality." It was this definition that I used as the basis for selecting places to include in the book.

Las Vegas is known so much for the bright, shiny hotels and casinos that adorn Las Vegas Boulevard, more commonly known as the famous "Strip," it can be easy to forget that surrounding that strip is an actual town—one where regular people live day-to-day lives, establish communities, and open businesses unique to this fascinating town. It is these places that I chose to include. Places with "recognized and enduring interest," those with "importance" and "quality," those that require a bit more investment to find than a walk down the Strip. However, trust me, that investment will not only be worth it, it'll be well rewarded.

Still, the Strip is one of the main reasons people come to Las Vegas and ignoring it didn't seem quite right. So I didn't. Several of the places I included in the book are located right on Las Vegas Boulevard, and many of these places are both iconic and so associated with Las Vegas that the book wouldn't be complete without them. Besides the fifty places I chose to write full stories about, there are many other vintage spots that are mentioned throughout the book. So if you flip through the table of contents and don't automatically see a place you thought should have been included, fret not, your favorite might just be one of those vintage spots. If after reviewing the vintage spots, you still don't find it, my apologies.

This book has been so much fun to write and it has taught me some very important lessons, the biggest of which is this: If you want a business to last, you'd better surround yourself with great people and see those people not as employees, but as family. I hope this book brings you as much enjoyment reading it as it brought me writing it and that it gives you a unique view of this amazing little town that so many of us call home. I hope too that it inspires you to seek out and visit these places, whether you're a resident or a visitor, before their books close for good. Let's just hope that's a long way off. Enjoy!

ATOMIC LIQUORS

917 FREMONT ST. • LAS VEGAS, NV 89101

(702) 982-3000 • ATOMICLASVEGAS.COM

A Roof with a View

On November 12, 1951, Las Vegas made the cover of *Life* magazine, but not for its showgirls, casinos, or even its ninety-nine-cent shrimp cocktails. It made the cover with a photo of an atomic cloud that was visible behind the neon signs of the Pioneer and Las Vegas Club downtown. When America entered the Atomic Age in the early 1950s, Las Vegas grabbed hold and went right along for the ride. At the time the United States government established the Nevada Test Site in January of 1951, Las Vegas was still a very small town. The mega-casinos that would eventually fill the Las Vegas Strip were still but a dream. Most casinos and businesses were located either on or right off Fremont Street in what is now downtown Las Vegas.

Although the government tried to conceal the tests it conducted a short sixty-five miles northwest of the city, the bright lights and distinctive clouds the aboveground explosions created were hard to hide. Once Las Vegas found out about the tests, it embraced them. Hotels organized picnics, restaurants added atomic burgers to their menus, and some places created atomic cocktails. The Las Vegas Chamber of Commerce even produced a calendar of scheduled blasts for tourists and, as it turns out, locals. It was during these blasts that patrons of a bar on Fremont Street, drinks in hand, took to the roof of the small brick building to watch the blasts. At the time in Las Vegas there was little that would impede visibility between the bar and the blast site. This made the little store one of the best seats on the house. The activity became so popular that the place was christened Atomic Liquors in 1952 by its owner.

Atomic Liquors got its start way back in 1921 when Helen, age four, and Stella, age two, stepped off a train in Las Vegas with their mother, Virginia. Not one to shy away from work, Virginia took a job as a cook for the Union Pacific Railroad and later as caretaker to John Busteed, an elderly Nevada judge. Virginia worked for Busteed up until he died, inheriting, as part of Busteed's estate, a piece of property on Fremont Street between 9th and 10th streets. Virginia used Busteed's gift to open a gas station and an auto court, which she appropriately named Virginia's Auto Court. As her businesses grew successful, Virginia wanted to open a cafe. While she had met and married Jack Barrett, both Virginia and Jack were getting a little long in the tooth to manage all their businesses so they asked Virginia's daughter Stella to consider helping. Stella had moved to Niagara Falls and married a man named Joe Sobchik. The two took Stella's parents up on their offer, moved to Las Vegas, and Virginia's Café was born.

After a time Joe tired of cooking and was looking for an easier source of income, so when the opportunity to purchase a liquor-store license became available, Joe and Stella jumped in. Virginia's Café became a liquor store. Several years later, a pour license once owned by the Lido Lounge also became available. Joe wasted no time in purchasing the license, which allowed them to add a bar onto the liquor store—eventually becoming the oldest freestanding bar in Las Vegas. As a result of the liquor store/bar combination, Las Vegas created a new classification and with it a new license, which they called the tavern license. Atomic Liquors was issued license #00001.

Over the years Atomic Liquors served the likes of Dean Martin, Frank Sinatra, Barbara Streisand, and the Smothers Brothers. Streisand established a friendship with Stella and stopped at the bar every time she was in town to visit her friend, have a drink, and play some pool. Atomic Liquors stayed open twenty-four hours a day, making it a popular hangout for casino workers and entertainers getting off late—and early—shifts. An episode of the original *Twilight Zone*, as well as movies such as Clint Eastwood's *The Gauntlet* and Martin Scorsese's *Casino* were filmed at the bar. You'll recognize the bar in the scene where Joe Pesci's character Nicky Santoro kills a man with a pen. Scorsese even used the adjacent garage as a production studio.

While the bar maintained its popularity, over the years it began to fall into disrepair, and then in October of 2010 Joe passed away. He was followed by his beloved wife Stella only three months later. They were both ninety-one. That's when brothers Lance and Kent Johns, along with their partner—filmmaker Derek Stonebarger—stepped in. "I was just drawn to it," says Lance. "I saw that it had potential to come back." So the trio closed the place, refurbished it, and opened it up again a short two years later with the same name. The bar was an immediate hit, mainly because Lance and Kent worked very hard to preserve its history. "The place really resonates with people," says Lance. "Anyone who's been in town for a while knows about us."

Wherever possible the brothers left the place as it was. A curved soffit in the roof is original—although the city made them smooth out the popcorn ceiling over the bar. The red neon that lights up the soffit is also original. "It was there when we bought the place," says Lance. "Our electrician worked on it and got it to light back up." When the neon is turned on, it gives the bar an impressive rose-colored tint. Many of the items that were original to the place are still there. The original Las Vegas Liquor License and Nevada Sales Tax License still hang on the wall. There is a pool cue rack, complete with an assortment of cues, even though the pool tables have long since disappeared.

Vintage Spots

HUNTRIDGE TAVERN: EST. 1962

This tavern, which was visited by *Anthony Bourdain: Parts Unknown* in 2014, has been a Las Vegas locals' hangout since 1962. The small bar is famous for its barbecues, chili cookoffs, and volleyball parties that it held in the used-to-be-dirt parking lot. The bar is still going strong and according to bartender/manager Kate Alexander, "We're gonna be open for another fifty years."

1116 E. Charleston Blvd.; (702) 384-7377

DINO'S LOUNGE: EST. 1962

Originally called Ringside Liquors, the place was owned by gentleman gangster Eddie Trascher. In 1962 Ringside Liquors was bought by Rinaldo Dean "Dino" Bartolomucci, who turned the liquor store into a bar. It is now owned and operated by Dino's granddaughter Kristen Bartolo and is still catering to tourists and locals alike on the Las Vegas Strip.

1516 S. Las Vegas Blvd.; (702) 382-3894; dinoslv.com

There is also a collection of signs original to the business. One says Atomic Liquors Parking Only, while others say No Overnight Parking, and No RVs. One sign, which was designed to look hand-painted, warns that it is illegal to possess an open container of alcoholic beverage which was purchased in an original sealed or corked container within 1,000 feet of this establishment, by Las Vegas ordinance. Still another sign reminds patrons that all package sales are final, no exceptions.

Located on one wall are a collection of signs from the test site, a not-so-silent nod to a time in Las Vegas's past where people used to watch atomic blasts, without protective goggles, from the roof of a liquor store and cocktail lounge. A time when the government scientists assured the residents of Las Vegas that the harmful effects of the blasts would dissipate long before they made their way to Las Vegas—even though the blasts were often strong enough to shake

Las Vegas buildings and blow out windows. After Joe changed the name of the place to Atomic Liquors, he erected a large neon sign at the front of the building—a sign that remains proudly in place.

Joe and Stella had only one son, Ron, who grew up to become an aerospace engineer. When the couple died, their memorials were held at Atomic Liquors. And while Joe and Stella may be gone, their presence is still felt. The bathrooms have been remodeled to look like they would have in the 1950s and renamed Joe's and Stella's—Stella's is even painted her favorite pink. In addition, Joe continues to look over the place, not from above, but from below. No, Joe hasn't descended to the world of fire and pitchforks; when the bar was remodeled Lance and Kent found a safe in the floor. Inside the safe were several items, including Joe's sheriff card—the license needed to serve alcohol or work with food in Las Vegas. The plastic license had Joe's sunglasses-clad photo on it. Instead of pulling up the safe, the brothers decided to leave it in the floor, cover it with Plexiglas, and light it up. Now when you enter the bar you can look down on Joe and see him looking right back.

THE AUTO COLLECTION

3535 S. LAS VEGAS BLVD. • LAS VEGAS, NV 89109

(702) 794-3174 • AUTOCOLLECTIONS.COM

Gentlemen, Start Your Engines

Go to a car lot nowadays and all you'll find are the same boring vehicles. It's like one person designed a car and everybody else stole that very same design. All the Hondas look like all the Toyotas, which look like all the Nissans, which look like all the Fords, which look like all the Chevys. But it wasn't always that way. At one time in America automobiles had personality. They had rear fins, angled tails, and bullet fronts. They had shiny, chrome bumpers; sparkling, elaborate grills; and fancy, sculptural ornamentation on their hoods. Long before paint took its place, pinstriping was done with chrome pieces that stretched all the way down the side of the car. These cars were big, fast, and, well . . . beautiful.

If you long for the days when your car was as important a member of the family as, say, the dog, there's still one place you can go. The Auto Collection, located at the top of the Quad Resort and Casino's parking garage, is a 125,000-square-foot facility packed with vintage vehicles, many of which date back to the 1920s and '30s. Here you can find a 1923 Ahrens Fox fire truck, a 1936 BMW Cabriolet, a 1954 Nash-Healey LeMans coupe, a 1955 Chevrolet Cameo Carrier, and a 1957 Chrysler 300C convertible, and that is only the beginning.

The Auto Collection got its start in 1980 as the personal auto collection of Ralph Engelstad, the owner of the Asian-themed Imperial Palace (previously the Flamingo Capri). Engelstad placed his auto collection on the top floor of the Imperial Palace's parking garage, surrounded it with walls, and opened it to the public. In 1999 the auto collection was sold to The Auction, Inc., which has operated it ever

since. In 2005, after Engelstad's death, the Imperial Palace was sold to Harrah's, which was eventually bought out by Caesars Entertainment.

The Auto Collection is one of the few places left where you can find such a vast assembly of vintage automobiles. At one time or another, the collection has contained such notable vehicles as "Eleanor," the 1967 Fastback Ford Mustang driven by Nicolas Cage in the movie *Gone in Sixty Seconds*; the 1962 Lincoln Continental Towne Limousine used by President John F. Kennedy; and the 1919 Pierce Arrow Model 66 built for comedian Roscoe "Fatty" Arbuckle.

There are approximately 250 cars on any given day, although the number changes. This is because the Auto Collection isn't a museum, it's a showroom. "We sold fourteen cars in the last six days," says general manager Rob Williams. "This is the world's largest classic car showroom by far." That's right, not only can you see the car of your dreams here, you can take it home with you—that is, if you have enough money. Perhaps you want that 1954 Nash-Healey LeMans coupe; it'll set you back $350,000. Maybe a classic 1957 T-Bird is more your style. You can get a pink one in mint condition for the bargain price of only $65,000. Or if you've always wanted to own a 1958 Rolls-Royce Silver Cloud I, you can pick one up for a mere $1,250,000.

Of course, not every vehicle in the collection is for sale. Some remain in the showroom's permanent collection. One of those residents is a 1939 Horch 930V Phaeton. This vintage car is one of only three that were ever built and one of the two that still survive. If you want to see the other one, you have to go to England and ask Oliver Bentfort if you can see his. Another car in the permanent collection is the 1974 Hong-Qi CA-770 Red Flag Limousine. This shiny black car has a massive chrome grill, white-wall tires, and suicide doors. The Hong-Qi brand of limousine is not only China's first manufactured car line, this actual limousine is the very first collector car ever to be exchanged between China and the United States.

Probably the most famous vehicle in the collection is the 1939 Chrysler Royal Sedan that talk-show host Johnny Carson drove to his senior prom. Sometime after Carson left home, his father—who owned the car—sold it. However, after Carson achieved his fame, the host of *The Tonight Show* tracked down the sedan, bought it back, and had it restored. In 1994 he sold the sedan to the Imperial Palace to be placed in its auto collection. The sale price? One dollar.

While most of the cars in the collection are for sale, some of them have grown so attached they never want to leave. Take, for example, the 1922 Renault Model 40 Kellner Town Car. This black beauty looks like something you'd expect the *Munsters* to drive. It is a combination of a horse-drawn carriage and an automobile. The driver—with the steering wheel on the right side—sits at the front of the vehicle in an area open to the elements. The passengers, however, sit in a rear coachlike section encased with a leather-covered roof. Wide running boards allow passengers to step up onto the Town Car as they get in, and there is even a long chrome handle on the side of the roof that can be held to ensure balance. The twelve-spoke rims are made of wood—that's right, wood. A spare tire sits to the side of the car toward the front, right behind the engine.

The Town Car was once part of the Brucker Collection of Los Angeles, California, before the Brucker family sold it to the MovieWorld: Cars of the Stars museum, which opened in 1970. When the museum closed only three years later, the Town Car was sold several times, eventually making its way to the Imperial Palace Auto Collection in December of 1984. In 1985 the Imperial Palace paid Mike Fennel—one of the world's premier car restorers—to restore the

Town Car. It took Fennel the better part of a year to do so, and once completed the car was returned to the Imperial Palace's collection, where it stayed until 1999, when it was sold. In 2007 the Town Car returned to the collection and was sold again that same year. However, undaunted, the Town Car again found its way back to the auto collection in 2013, where it currently resides.

While the collection is a showroom, it's not a typical showroom where you can sit in the cars or take one out for a test drive. Every car in the collection is cordoned off with velvet ropes stopping you from getting closer than four or five feet from the car. There's no touching in this showroom. Signs are placed in front of each car giving a description and, where appropriate, the list price.

The best part of the Auto Collection is that it's always changing, because the cars are continuously being sold. You may find a 1957 Bel Air Convertible on one visit and a 1976 Eldorado Bicentennial Convertible with only 2,000 original miles on your next. Either way, as you walk around the Auto Collection, crooned to by Elvis, you're transported back to days of yore. Whether you climbed into the passenger seat of that Nomad with your granddad to get a haircut, piled into the back of the family wagon and headed to the drive-in, or cruised the main drag in a 1960s muscle car, the memories of your youth are all assembled into one convenient spot. "We try to have something for everybody," says Rob. And, if you didn't find it on this visit, you can always come back next time. Your dream car will be waiting.

BATTISTA'S HOLE IN THE WALL

4041 LINQ LN. • LAS VEGAS, NV 89109
(702) 732-1424 • BATTISTASLASVEGAS.COM

An Old-World Atmosphere

*L*as Vegas is well known for its past involvement with crook-nosed gangsters dressed in expensive pinstriped suits, skimming money from the count room of casinos such as the Golden Nugget, the Desert Inn, the Stardust, the Fremont, the Hacienda, and the Flamingo. And while the mob has long ago left Las Vegas, you'd still expect some of its influence to linger—meaning you wouldn't be surprised to find an Italian restaurant on almost every corner. Sadly, this is not the case. In fact, finding a good Italian restaurant in Las Vegas is about as hard as leaving Las Vegas with more money in your pocket than you had when you got here. Finding an Italian restaurant that makes you feel like you're on Prince Street in Boston or Little Italy in New York is a tall order indeed. That is, unless you slip behind the Flamingo Hotel and Casino and go to Battista's Hole in the Wall.

"It's a fun, old-world atmosphere," says Doug Morgan, Battista's general manager and maître d'. "People like the vintage atmosphere." When you step into Battista's, vintage is exactly what you get. You enter the restaurant through a door shaped like a large wine barrel. Once inside, you find you've left Las Vegas and stepped into another world. Hanging from the ceiling are all shapes and sizes of wine bottles. There are also baskets, license plates, plastic grapes, cloves of garlic, and soccer banners, all intermixed with the lights hanging from the ceiling. Covering almost every square inch of the walls are photos of famous people who have eaten at the restaurant, many of whom had their photos taken with Battista Locatelli, the one-time owner and namesake of Battista's Hole in the Wall.

Battista Locatelli was born in Bergamo, Italy, an Italian town in Northern Italy near Lake Como. Battista had an Italian mother and an American father, giving him dual citizenship. In 1949, at the age of eighteen, Battista moved to America, landing in Santa Cruz, California. It was there that he met his future wife, Rio. After the couple married, they moved to Los Angeles where Battista got a job as a waiter and bartender at La Scala and later at the Bel Air Hotel in Beverly Hills. Besides his skill behind the bar, Battista also had vocal skills. He was a tenor, singing part-time whenever he could. While working as a bartender at the Bel Air Hotel, Battista met many stars, some of whom—after they heard his voice—asked him to perform at their private functions.

At thirty-eight, Battista got a singing gig in Las Vegas, so he and Rio packed up their four children and moved. Unfortunately, before he could even start work, the singing gig fell through, leaving Battista with little choice but to fall back on what he knew: waiting tables. One day while looking through the local paper, Rio found an ad for a closing restaurant called The Dive. The owners were looking for someone to take over the lease. She showed the ad to Battista and on May 1, 1970, the couple opened a sandwich shop in the tiny space that was once The Dive. "It was a real hole in the wall," Battista once said of

Vintage Spot
BOOTLEGGER ITALIAN BISTRO: EST. 2001

While this Italian restaurant has only been open for close to fourteen years, it is owned by a family of restaurateurs whose Las Vegas roots go back to 1955, when Albert "Al" and Maria Perry opened the Venetian Pizzeria on Fremont Street. They would open two more restaurants—the Venetian Restaurant in 1960 and the Bootlegger Ristorante in 1972. While those three restaurants have all eventually closed, the family legacy still holds strong in the very capable hands of their daughter Lorraine—though ninety-year-old "Mama Maria" still oversees the kitchen.

**7700 S. Las Vegas Blvd.; (702) 736-4939;
bootleggerlasvegas.com**

the space, which was only able to accommodate fourteen people at a time.

Rio cooked while Battista ran the front of the house. "In the beginning they only served breakfast and lunch," says Doug, who started working at the restaurant when he was fifteen. Doug lived across the street from the Locatellis and even helped Battista and Rio clean out The Dive in preparation for opening Battista's. While working the front, Battista would often sing to the guests. This, combined with their Dago Burger (pronounced "Day Go"), made the restaurant an instant hit.

As things progressed, Battista began getting visits from his Hollywood friends, such as Johnny Weissmuller, Sergio Franchi, and Robert Goulet. Every time one of them would visit the restaurant, Battista offered to make them famous by taking a photo of them and putting it on the wall of the restaurant. "I'd like to make you famous," he'd tell them. "I'll put your picture on my wall." There are so many photos on the walls now, it's almost impossible to see the wood paneling behind them. One of Battista's frequent guests was Betty Grable. In fact, when Grable died in 1973, Battista sang at her funeral.

While Battista's Hole in the Wall may give you that old-world feeling, it isn't a completely traditional Italian restaurant. That is made evident by the head of an Alaskan moose resting on the wall by the hostess stand with a sign underneath that reads, MY NAME IS MOOOSO- LINI. Next to the moose head is a yellow fire hydrant, and across the opening that leads to the seating area is a barber pole. There is also a six-foot coffee grinder, the world's largest collection of miniature alcohol bottles, and signs scattered around the restaurant with say- ings such as, "It'sa nice to be important, but it'sa important to be nice."

As it turns out, entering Battista through a wine barrel is fitting because every meal at Battista's also comes with free house wine. Yes, that's right, free wine. Red or white, whichever you prefer. And not just one glass—you get free wine during your entire meal. "We're a favorite for large groups and parties," Battista once said. But it's not the free wine that brings people back night after night. It's the service and, of course, the food.

While Battista's has grown over the years—it can now seat close to three hundred people—and Battista himself has retired, the res- taurant that still holds his name has remained true to the original atmosphere started by Battista and Rio more than forty years ago. The menu is simple, mounted on large boards in every room, and in a time of expensive food and à la carte menus, Battista's still believes in giving value for your dollar. That is why, besides the wine, every meal still comes with minestrone soup or Italian salad, garlic bread, a pasta side, and homemade cappuccino. It is also probably the only place in Las Vegas where you can eat an Italian meal while being serenaded by an accordion player under the watchful eye of a water buffalo.

BONANZA GIFT AND SOUVENIR SHOPS

2440 S. LAS VEGAS BLVD. • LAS VEGAS, NV 89104
(702) 385-7359 • WORLDSLARGESTGIFTSHOP.COM

If It's in Stock, We Have It

Those words set the tone for the store that bills itself as "the world's largest gift shop." "The sign was featured on the *Ellen DeGeneres* show," says manager Angie Hurt. "They called first to verify that it really said that." It does. The statement is set proudly in large red letters on the outside of the store, right next to the store's proclamation of size.

Whether or not the store is actually the "world's largest" may be up for debate. What is certain is this: If you're looking for any type of Las Vegas souvenir, there's no better place in the world to go than the Bonanza Gift and Souvenir Shops. The Bonanza Gift Shop is not only big, it's also fun, probably because it doesn't take itself too seriously. When Afrojack and Steve Aoki secretly recorded their video for "No Beef featuring Miss Palmer" on a cell phone without the store's permission, the gift shop didn't get upset. Instead they turned it into a marketing opportunity by prominently featuring the gifts purchased in the video.

While it has been in business since 1972 in different places, the gift shop has been in its current location for more than thirty years. It was opened by Bruce Morris, who originated the concept of putting gift shops in Las Vegas casinos. In 1980 he moved the shop to the corner of Las Vegas Boulevard and Sahara Avenue, the site of the oldest strip mall in Las Vegas. The mall, built by Richard Tam in 1950, was originally a supermarket with small shops on the side. At one time the mall contained stores like Garwood Van's Musicland. Van was the

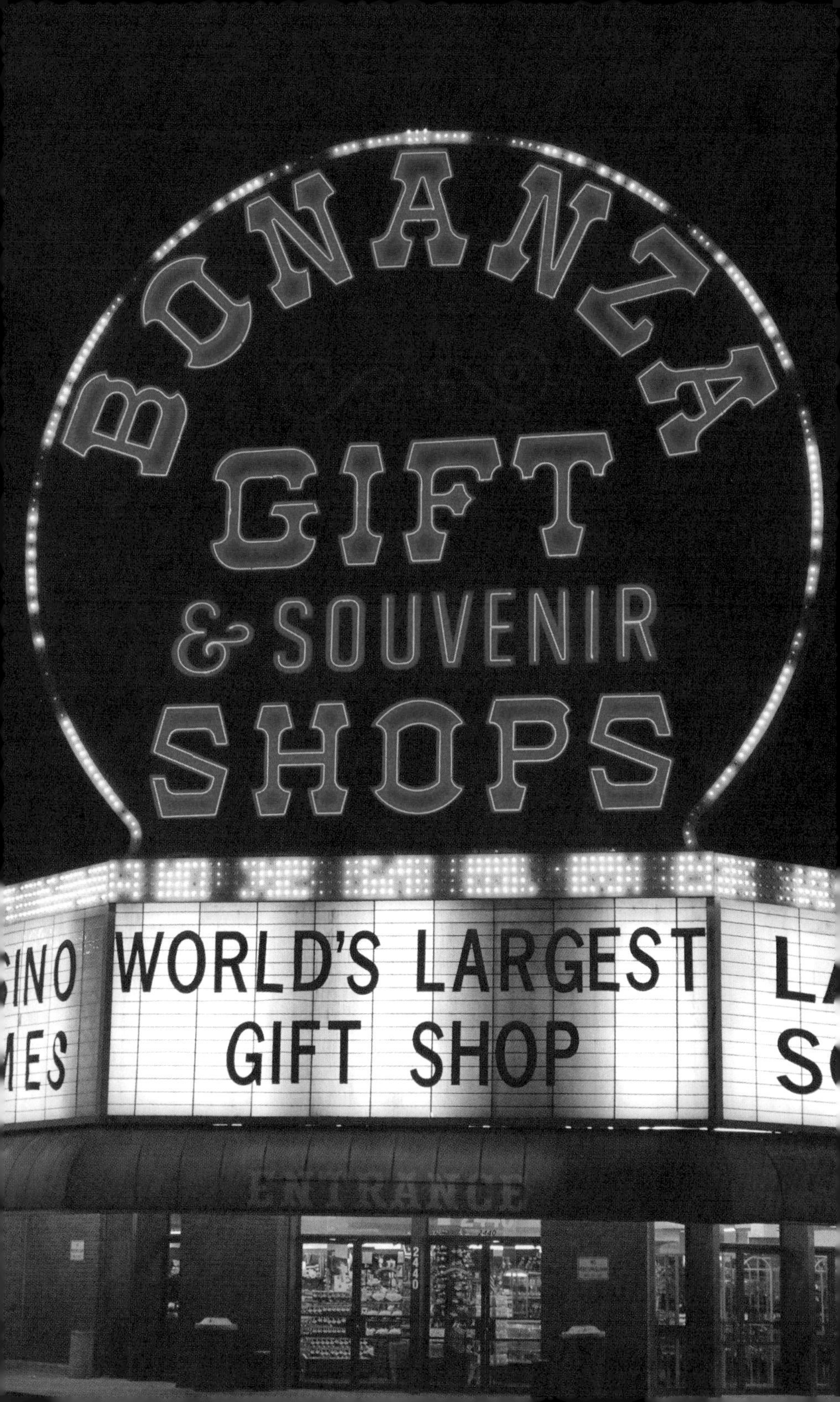
BONANZA
GIFT
& SOUVENIR
SHOPS
WORLD'S LARGEST
GIFT SHOP
2440

leader of the house band for both the El Rancho across the street and The Last Frontier when entertainers like Ronald Reagan headlined the casino. When Van opened the music store in 1959, it was the only place to buy record albums in Las Vegas. The mall also contained a pharmacy, a clothing store called Charlie Shelton's Rowel, and David Ming's Import Shop.

The mall was eventually the site of the Honest John Casino, before that was replaced by the Big Wheel Casino, then the Centerfold Casino, and finally the Jolly Trolley Restaurant, Saloon and Dining Depot. In 1979 porn star Marilyn Chambers danced completely naked in a one-woman play called "The Sex Surrogate" at the Jolly Trolley. "This is the floor where Marilyn Chambers danced naked," Angie says, pointing it out on our tour of the gift shop. The wood dance floor is still in place, as is the stained-glass ceiling. Only now, instead of promoting a naked dancer, the area showcases luggage.

Another little bit of history is the Ferris wheel that used to revolve on the roof of the Big Wheel Casino. Guests of the casino could go up to the roof and ride the wheel—which wasn't a very long ride. The frame still exists on the ceiling where it was originally. But now, instead of supporting a Ferris wheel, it supports the round Bonanza Gift and Souvenir Shops sign.

The gift shop has the standard gifts you'd expect to find in a gift shop—shot glasses, mugs, ashtrays, key chains, bottle openers, and magnets all with various incarnations of the Las Vegas theme. However, it also has some vintage gifts you may not expect. One of the best finds in this sometimes kitschy, sometimes classy gift shop are the note cards that feature photos of Las Vegas's past. Here you can find a photo of the inside of the long-ago-demolished Arizona Club from 1905, a shot of downtown Las Vegas from 1940, a view of the Desert Inn swimming pool from 1950, an aerial view of the Flamingo Hotel from 1952, or a photo of the Horseshoe Club from 1953. You can also find a shot of the Sands Hotel and Casino's famous floating craps game—a craps game that took place in the swimming pool. If you're a little on the daring side, you can find note cards featuring the popular topless showgirls of the 1960s.

If you perhaps fell in love with the iconic WELCOME TO LAS VEGAS sign on your trip to our little town, for only $49.99 you can take home a scaled-down version of the sign that lights up just like the real one. The world's largest gift shop is also the place to purchase Elvis-related gifts. Positioned next to the alien gifts is all manner of Elvis merchandise. Here you can find a Heartbreak Hotel street sign, Elvis wigs, and glasses complete with sideburns, as well as a sign that says, WHAT HAPPENS IN VEGAS STARTED IN GRACELAND. If you want a more personal gift, you can buy a replica of Elvis's Tennessee driver's license as a key chain, or, if you prefer, a magnet. You can also find various Elvis T-shirts, including one that shows him in his famous white jumpsuit in front of the International Hotel where he made his triumphant return to Las Vegas.

At the Bonanza Gift Shop you can purchase canceled cards from such iconic Las Vegas casinos as the Tropicana, Circus Circus, Binion's, Harrah's, and the Flamingo. You can buy fake gaming chips, a miniature slot machine, touch-screen video poker games, and even your own sixteen-inch deluxe roulette wheel set. If blackjack is more your thing, you can even purchase a mini blackjack table.

While there are tens of thousands of gifts waiting to be purchased at the Bonanza Gift Shop, there is one gift more famous, more vintage Las Vegas, than all the other gifts combined: the dice clock. Just as it sounds, the dice clock is a clock with dice where the numbers should be. It has been a Las Vegas staple since the '60s and is almost as well known as ninety-nine-cent shrimp cocktails, topless showgirls, or doubling down on a pair of tens. The best part about the dice clock is that it's the center of an ongoing Las Vegas controversy. Who invented the dice clock?

Depending on who you ask, the clock was created by either standup comic and musician Reve White or Steve Miller, son of Harold Miller who owned Miller Novelty Co. What is known is that the younger Miller was the first to create clocks made from the canceled dice of actual Las Vegas casinos. Miller took a piece of black plastic with a curved bottom, added gold hands and a battery block motor, and affixed dice where the numbers should be. He then attached the words "Fabulous Las Vegas" in gold to the clock.

Each number position has two dice, except for the "1" position, which only has one die. Miller also attached gold line graphics of a slot machine, a pair of dice, and two cards—an ace and a jack, which together equal 21. Miller originally showed the clock to his father, who thought it was the stupidest thing he had ever seen. However, the elder Miller changed his tune when Paula Peterson, manager of the Westward Ho's gift shop, gave Miller a thousand pairs of dice with which to make clocks.

The dice clock caught on and Miller was soon getting fifteen dollars a clock. Expanding his business, Miller got canceled dice from every casino that would sell to him—paying twenty-five cents a pair. If the casino wouldn't sell their dice, Miller paid pit bosses, security officers, or whoever he could to get the dice. While Miller's original clock was black plastic, dice clocks have graduated to various colors of plastic, including red, blue, gray, cream, sparkling purple, and even wood tones. "We sell ten to twenty thousand of these every year," says Angie of the dice clocks. Little has changed since dice clocks were first introduced in 1960. If you truly want a vintage souvenir, the dice clock is for you. And the good news is you can still buy the original bent plastic design or, if you prefer a more modern look, you can buy the flat design which can be hung on the wall. Either way, if it's in stock, Bonanza Gift and Souvenir Shops has it!

BOULDER DAM HOTEL

1305 ARIZONA ST. • BOULDER CITY, NV 89005
(702) 293-3510 • BOULDERDAMHOTEL.COM

The Hotel that Almost Wasn't

W hen Secretary of the Interior Ray Lyman Wilbur built Boulder City, its standout building was by far the Boulder Dam Hotel, an elegant three-story hotel that served as an oasis for tourists, dignitaries, and government officials. This is easy to believe when walking into the historic building. The foyer is made of rich southern gum paneling that is original to the building. A black grand piano sits in front of a paneled wall and the entire foyer is full of 1930s-era chairs, couches, and tables. Any walls that aren't covered in paneling are painted white, and green drapes hang high over tall windows, two of which stand guard on either side of a large fireplace at the back of the room. The decorative wood reception and check-in desk rests to the left of the foyer adjacent to the stairs, which are also built from the same southern gum.

The hotel has the classic style of the 1930s, but still manages to offer all the comforts expected by any modern traveler. However, Boulder City, Nevada, is a town that shouldn't exist and the Boulder City Hotel—even though it is now on the *National Register of Historic Places*—almost didn't. On December 30, 1930, President Calvin Coolidge authorized the building of a dam to tame the mighty Colorado River and produce energy for the inhabitants of Nevada, California, and Arizona. Wilbur, who was in charge of the dam's construction, loathed Las Vegas and had no intention of allowing his workers to live or even socialize with its incorrigible citizens. Wilbur was put off by Las Vegas's flagrant defiance of Prohibition laws and its embracement of prostitution. He saw Las Vegas as a dirty little town whose

residents were concerned only with the pursuit of pleasure. So he decided to build a town of his own, a short six miles from Boulder Canyon (the site of the dam), but far enough away from Sin City to be free of its corrupting influences.

Wilbur saw his town, which he christened Boulder City, as "a layout which will probably serve as a model in town planning for years to come." He planned to build a town hall, school, garage, dormitory and guesthouse, auditorium, administration building, swimming pool, playground, and seventy-five "cottages" for his employees. He had a two-million-dollar budget and he expected the town to become the new home of close to three thousand people—more than half the size of nearby Las Vegas. The difference, of course, was that his town would allow none of the vices that ran rampant in Sin City. There would be no alcohol, no gambling, and definitely no prostitution.

Wilbur's dreams of Boulder City becoming a "sizable tourist town" with a main transcontinental highway coming in from Arizona were coming to fruition; however, something was missing. If tourists, dignitaries, and government officials were going to come to the new Boulder City, a hotel was needed. So, in 1932, with construction of the dam well underway, plans began for the building of a seventy-four-room hotel in the heart of downtown Boulder City. The Boulder Inn, as it was slated to be called, was the brainchild of hoteliers W. F. Grey and his wife, Virginia Lamberson-Grey, who hired local architect L. Henry Smith to design a two-story, "fireproof" hotel.

"Sounds too good to be true," wrote the local newspaper. "A first-class hotel capable of caring for large parties of visitors has been the crying need of the community. The hotel, if built as planned at present, will be larger than the New Apache hotel in Las Vegas. Mr. and Mrs. Grey are to be commended for their initiation of this worthwhile project." The newspaper reported that the building was scheduled to be completed by September of 1932. But while the Greys had great intentions, their plans never seemed to take hold. "The lessees have just given us the unwelcome information that it is impossible to raise the required sum and that the enterprise must be abandoned," reported the newspaper in August of 1932.

Seizing the opportunity, Paul Stewart Webb, known as "Jim" to his friends, applied for, and was granted, a permit from the Bureau of Reclamation to build a hotel in Boulder City. Webb got together with Raymond Spilsbury and Austin Clark to build the structure they named the Boulder Dam Hotel. The trio hired architect Mort Wagner to design a Dutch colonial hotel with thirty-three rooms. "Each room had their own bathroom, which was unheard of at the time," says Laura Hutton, manager of the Boulder City/Hoover Dam Museum. "The hotel also had air conditioning, making it and the theater the only two buildings in Boulder City that had it."

From the moment it opened in 1933, the hotel was a huge success. Over the years it was visited by the likes of Bette Davis, Will Rogers, James Cagney, Henry Fonda, and Howard Hughes. "America's Sweetheart" Shirley Temple stayed there during a publicity stunt,

Vintage Spots

BOULDER CITY/HOOVER DAM MUSEUM: EST. 1981

Located inside the Boulder Dam Hotel is the Boulder City/ Hoover Dam Museum. The museum, which is dedicated to preserving the past and educating the future, tells the story of the Boulder Canyon Project "as it was experienced by the men and women who braved the desolation of the Southern Nevada desert to build Hoover Dam and Boulder City." The museum contains interactive displays and exhibits as well as photographs, artifacts, and oral histories.

1305 Arizona St.; (702) 294-1988; bcmha.org

RAILROAD PASS: EST. 1931

Just outside of nearby Boulder City, Nevada, the Railroad Pass has the distinction of being issued the fourth gaming license in the state of Nevada. The hotel was built in 1931 to serve the workers building the Hoover Dam and is the oldest operating casino in Nevada. It was so named because the railroad ran through the hills right behind the property, and while the railroad is long gone, the tunnels in the hills are still accessible as hiking trails. In addition, the hotel has a museum dedicated to the days of yesteryear, where you can find vintage photos, old slot machines, and Railroad Pass memorabilia.

2800 South Boulder Hwy.; (702) 294-5000; railroadpass.com

during which she visited a local school. Newspapers reported that she "went to school for the first time" in Boulder City.

In 1935 the Boulder Dam Hotel was expanded from its original thirty-three to eighty-six rooms in a sixty-thousand-dollar renovation. A restaurant was also added and both the hotel and the restaurant were included in the prestigious *Duncan Hines Adventures in Good Eating* and *Duncan Hines Adventures in Good Lodging* national guides. After the dam was completed, the employees should have returned to their homes throughout the United States and the town should have closed down, like so many western boomtowns. However, that wasn't the case. Instead of leaving, many of the dam workers stayed in town, making Boulder City their home. Unfortunately, the prosperity the hotel enjoyed early on didn't last, and by 1968 the hotel was closed. A year later it opened as a retirement home and operated as such until 1973. After that it experienced frequent closures and even fell victim to vandals.

However, ruin wasn't in the cards for this historic hotel. In 2005 the Boulder Dam Hotel was taken over completely by the Boulder City Museum and Historical Association and restored to its former glory. The hotel is now run by the nonprofit organization, which operates it as a functioning hotel, calling it a "living museum." The rooms have been reduced to twenty-one suites that are decorated just as they were when the hotel opened, or as close as possible. In fact, room 218 even has the same exact furniture that came with the room originally, thanks to a donation by Sara and Ralph Denton. "The furniture left the hotel, but eventually made its way back," says Laura with a bit of a smile.

While the hotel has a rich history, what really makes it unique is the love its caretakers have for the building. "There are a lot of people who not only work here, but volunteer here," says Laura. These workers and volunteers have a keen sense of history and what the hotel represents. As Laura explains, "We're always working to improve this place and keep it as original as possible." However, keeping a hotel built in 1933 original can pose its own set of problems. "It's a challenge," says head of maintenance and accommodations Isaac DeWolf. "I run into things that don't have instructions and I have to figure out how to fix them."

While it may have its moments, it's a job Isaac loves to do. He also showed his deep love for the hotel this year when he purchased a replica of an antique phone with his own money and placed it in room 223—called the Art Deco Room. "I found a company that used to make these phones originally," he says. "Now they make updated replicas of those phones." If you ask Isaac why he donated the phone to the hotel, he'll tell you, "I saw the phone and just knew it belonged in that room."

BUGSY SIEGEL'S MONUMENT AT THE FLAMINGO

3555 S. LAS VEGAS BLVD. • LAS VEGAS, NV 89109
(702) 733-3111 • FLAMINGOLASVEGAS.COM

A Success Unfulfilled

It's hard to talk about Las Vegas without mentioning many of its notable residents. There's Redd Foxx, Jerry Lewis, Wayne Newton, Nicolas Cage, Gladys Night, and, of course, Liberace. However, of all Las Vegas's famous residents, none is more notorious than Benjamin "Bugsy" Siegel. Son of Jewish immigrants, Siegel was born in Brooklyn, New York, in February 1906. He and his best friend Meyer Lansky made a name for themselves by putting together a string of illegal events called "floating craps games," so named because they were held in a different location every night.

During one of their late-night games, a local police sergeant by the name of Hearn stopped by the gathering, surprising the two men. While Lansky and Siegel were taken by surprise, the quick-thinking Lansky handed the dice to the sergeant, offering him very generous odds. Sergeant Hearn rolled the dice and won ten dollars—although his winnings didn't stop him from shutting the game down for the night. When Hearn left, an angry Siegel followed him. Siegel didn't like being made a fool of and hit Hearn over the head with a lead pipe, killing him.

The incident led to Siegel's famous nickname. When Lansky discovered that Siegel had the moxie to kill a cop over ten dollars, he said that Siegel was as crazy as a bedbug—a common term at the time. Siegel hated the name. "My friends call me Ben, strangers call me Mr. Siegel, and guys I don't like call me Bugsy, but not to my face," he was noted as saying. But whether or not Siegel liked the name,

it stuck, mainly because of Siegel's infamous temper. When he was mad his voice would get very soft and, according to his attorney Greg Bautzer, "His blue eyes would turn a slate grey color."

While Siegel and Lansky made a name for themselves in organized crime, Siegel was becoming more noted for his temper than anything else. By 1937 Lucky Luciano, boss of the syndicate, decided it was time to send Siegel to the west coast so that Siegel could escape the wrath of his enemies and avoid the numerous contracts that had reportedly been taken out on him. At the time, Las Vegas was still a small desert town. Gambling had been legalized only six years before and casinos were just starting to take a foothold in the tiny town. Luciano, with the help of Lansky, had managed to work his way into three properties on Fremont Street. While they were satisfied with their progress, they wanted to get more involved with the race and sports book operations, so they sent Siegel and Moe Sedway to investigate. Siegel helped the syndicate take a greater control over the race and sports book, until eventually they had a complete monopoly.

Though Siegel had a temper, he also had a very appealing side. Siegel was handsome and quite the gentleman. "I've never met a more courtly, a more gentlemanly man in my life," recalled singer Kay Starr. "I thought to myself, 'Well, if this is a gangster, I'd like to know more of them.'" Siegel had a fascination with the movie industry and harbored dreams of becoming a star in his own right. Siegel worked out of California, but made frequent trips to Las Vegas to check on the syndicate's interests. Instead of staying at the smaller, less-sophisticated casinos downtown, Siegel was a frequent guest in one of the two outlying casinos, the El Rancho and the Last Frontier. It was during a stay in the El Rancho that Siegel came up with the idea for a luxurious resort hotel and casino. Figuring he could easily compete with the El Rancho and the Last Frontier, he decided to place his resort on Highway 91—a highway that would eventually be known as Las Vegas Boulevard, or, more famously, "the Strip."

To Siegel's great luck, a property was already being built on Highway 91. Billy Wilkerson, a known gambler, had put more money than he could afford into a resort that he wasn't able to finish. Siegel was able to convince Lansky that the resort would be a success and with Lansky's approval, Siegel came on board with Wilkerson and soon

Vintage Spots

LEGENDS IN CONCERT: EST. 1983

Bugsy's monument isn't the only vintage find at the Flamingo. The hotel and casino is also home to the longest-running celebrity tribute show in the world. Here you can find such notables as Old Blue Eyes, Elvis, Sammy, and Marilyn performing nightly alongside Bobby Darin, Frankie Valli, Liberace, and Judy Garland, all hosted by Ed Sullivan.

**3555 S. Las Vegas Blvd.; (702) 777-7776;
legendsinconcert.com**

THE TROPICANA LAS VEGAS: EST. 1957

While many of the casinos in Las Vegas have either been imploded or have changed names, a few of the original casinos still exist. One of those is the Tropicana Las Vegas. Started in 1957, the property housed the famous French-style topless revue the *Folies Bergère* until 2009 when the show had its final performance. The show, which made showgirls famous, was the last bastion of the famous old-time Las Vegas shows.

3801 Las Vegas Blvd. South; (702) 379-2222; troplv.com

THE RIVIERA: EST. 1955

When the Riviera opened it featured an Olympic-sized swimming pool, eighteen table games, and 116 slot machines. The Clover Showroom featured Liberace on its opening night, an event hosted by actress Joan Crawford. While the hotel has changed owners numerous times, it has remained in its original location for almost sixty-five years.

**2901 Las Vegas Blvd. South; (702) 734-5110;
rivierahotel.com**

THE PALACE STATION: EST. 1976

This off-the-Strip locals' casino has been in operation since 1976. It started as simply The Casino, before being changed to the Bingo Palace a year later when the owners added bingo to the property. In 1984 the name was officially changed to Palace Station when the property was remodeled with a railroad theme. It is one of the few family-owned casinos left in the valley.

2411 W. Sahara; (702) 367-2411; palacestation.sclv.com

took over the property. By 1945 Siegel had managed to raise one million dollars toward the building of his new Flamingo Club, later changed to Flamingo Hotel for licensing purposes.

However, building a resort in the desert proved more complicated than Siegel expected. Building costs were continually rising as the construction schedule kept getting pushed back. Impatient with not seeing a quick return on their investment, Luciano insisted Siegel open the Flamingo before it was ready. With pressure from Luciano and against his own judgment, Siegel opened the resort the day after Christmas in 1946. The seventy-seven-room hotel had a health club, pool, tennis courts, a golf course, shops, showrooms, and stables for forty horses. Siegel couldn't have picked a worse day to open his hotel. California was experiencing a wet, rainy December and those conditions prevented many of Siegel's Hollywood connections from making the trip to Las Vegas. In addition, many of the rooms weren't completed, forcing several of Siegel's guests to take rooms at the El Rancho and the Last Frontier. Losses were so heavy that after two weeks, Siegel, unable to pay his staff, was forced to close the doors.

Luciano was furious. "There was no doubt in Meyer's mind that Bugsy had skimmed this dough from his building budget," he wrote in his memoirs, "and he was sure that Siegel was preparing to skip as well as skim, in case the roof was gonna fall in on him." Siegel's fate was sealed. Six months after the opening of his beloved hotel, in June of 1947, Benjamin "Bugsy" Siegel was shot in the head and chest while sitting on the couch reading the paper in the California bungalow he shared with his girlfriend Virginia Hill. Even though Siegel's demise was front-page news across the country, only five people, all family, attended his funeral. Not one of Siegel's new Hollywood friends found the time to attend. It was a sad, embarrassing end for a man who had such grandiose visions of himself.

But while Siegel's ending may have come before its time, the casino he started has lived on. It reopened on March 1, 1947 and though it has changed hands many times, it has remained open for nearly seventy years. Although Siegel's friends may have abandoned him in his time of need, the casino, which Siegel would never see reach its full potential, has not forgotten its original benefactor. Out by the pool, near the wedding chapel, stands a stone monument with a brass plaque called the "Bugsy" Building. The plaque bears both

Siegel's likeness and a view of what his beloved hotel looked like when it opened in 1946.

Interestingly enough, Siegel built a suite on the top floor of the hotel to protect himself against a possible attack. The windows were made of bulletproof materials and while there was only one entrance, there were five escape routes—one of which was a ladder that went from the hallway closet to a basement tunnel, leading to an underground garage. Unfortunately, Siegel's placement of the suite turned out to be a tragic miscalculation.

CHAMPAGNES CAFÉ

3557 S. MARYLAND PKWY. • LAS VEGAS, NV 89169

(702) 737-1699

The Good Ol' Days of Las Vegas

Champagnes Café isn't your typical Las Vegas haunt. First of all, it isn't a cafe, and second, they don't serve champagne. What they do offer is a unique link to Las Vegas's past—one where the Rat Pack was the hottest act in town and the mob ruled with an iron fist. "We used to come here after hours when there was nothing else open," says former hit man and mob enforcer Frank Cullotta. "This used to be a real nice area." Looking at the place, you might think its late-night enticement centered on the fact that the joint has both a front and a rear entrance—or exit, depending how you look at it. But Frank has a much simpler answer: "The cops didn't know we were here." That was in the 1970s when Cullotta was part of the famous Hole in the Wall Gang, with Tony "the Ant" Spilotro. The gang got its name due to its habit of cutting holes in the walls of the businesses they robbed, or burned, to bypass the alarm system. Champagnes Café was a common hangout for mobsters back then and it's easy to see why, because Champagnes has a decor that is, in a word, unique.

Walking through the red front door, you feel like you've just stepped inside an iconic 1960s Las Vegas showroom or possibly a 1930s speakeasy. A wood bar, complete with padded chair-style stools, runs almost the entire length of the small room. Behind the bar, standing like soldiers at attention, rest rows of alcohol bottles in all shapes and sizes. The bottles are positioned in front of mirrored glass made to look like marble. It is the only area of the bar that is well lit, and the light draws your eyes right to it as soon as you walk in the door.

Once your eyes adjust to the dark, you'll find padded leather booths running along the wall opposite the bar. The booths are old, but there is still enough cushion for even the most discriminating of bottoms. Black tables laminated with faux leather sit between the booths and red 1960s-era chairs. Every ceiling light is equipped with a red lightbulb, giving the entire bar a rose tint. And while all of this adds to Champagnes' ambience, there is one thing that gets more publicity than anything else in the entire place—the wallpaper. "The wallpaper is the original from 1966," says Kenny Bressers, Champagnes' current owner and sometimes morning bartender. The red velvet paper covered with a fancy decorative gold pattern is on every wall, including the bathroom—though in there the red has faded a bit. "That wallpaper is one of our best advertising tools," says Kenny. "We've never changed it and we have no plans to."

Champagnes Café has its own style and charm, and sitting at one of its booths or ordering a drink at the bar you can almost picture what it was like when the Rat Pack came in late at night for a few drinks. Which was, in fact, once the case. "Back then Sammy couldn't drink in the casinos," says Kenny, referring to the 1960s rule that not only prevented black entertainers from booking rooms in the casinos they performed in, but also prevented them from even walking around the place and having a look. "Even back then they were welcome here," he says. Once they were done performing at the Sands, Sammy Davis Jr. and the rest of the Rat Pack used to come into Champagnes Café, and sitting in these booths they must have felt right at home. "People come here for the history, for that old feel," Kenny explains, adding, "This is a great place to get the Las Vegas experience without paying a lot of money."

In fact, as the staff at Champagnes will tell you, you never know just who you might see coming in that red door. "We get customers from all over the world," says bartender Donna McCue, who adds that Champagnes is also the hangout of many Strip performers. "We had the cast of *Absinth* in the other night," says Kenny, speaking of the show currently playing at Caesars Palace. *Bad Ink* did an episode at Champagnes, as did the Travel Channel. Movies have even been filmed at Champagnes Café. Stephen Baldwin filmed *Stop Traffick* there, with Baldwin himself working behind the bar.

If you long for the old days when the mob had a strong influence in Las Vegas, Champagnes is your place. It is not at all uncommon to see some old gangsters sitting in the booths or even doing book signings at Champagnes Café. This was the case with Frank Cullotta and Antonio Raimundo "Tony" Montana who both had book signings on the same night. Frank arrived—white fedora on his head and cigars in his shirt pocket—in the company of two buxom beauties less than half his age. As Dean croons over speakers in the background, Frank's two companions take their seats in one of the padded booths, while Frank readies himself for the book signing. Frank is very cordial as he greets his fans. If you're a guy he shakes your hand, if you're a gal he hugs you, and if you ask nicely, he even takes a photo with you.

Tony, who looks more like what you'd expect a mobster to look like, sits next to Frank's companions. He wears a black coat, a dark shirt, black pants, and sports a newsboy-style cap. Tony also has on dark glasses that make seeing infinitely more difficult in a place where the lights are already so dim it's a strain to see anyway. Like Frank, Tony is willing to sign books, but he's also willing to tell you the history of Champagnes, something he knows very well.

"It used to be the Inner Circle," says Tony, who is also a former member of the Hole in the Wall Gang. "Then it became Huey's and Jerry's East, before it was sold to Tony Champagnes who died here in the office." Tony, whose name was borrowed by Al Pacino in the movie *Scarface*, remembers Huey's fondly. "They had the best burgers in town," he says, adding that it was Huey who was responsible for Champagnes' current decor.

One thing that no one is able to tell you is when the doors first opened. Some claim the year to be 1964, while others put it as far back as 1961. "It's kind of a mystery when it opened," says Kenny. "It just adds to the mystique of the place." Kenny is set on making sure Champagnes' atmosphere remains as historic as ever. One of the ways he does this is by hosting a once-a-month event called Music, Martinis and Memories. The party is a celebration of vintage Vegas culture and attire. People come dressed up in vintage clothing, drink, and mingle all while music from the '40s and '50s plays in the background. "It's a throwback to the old cocktail parties," says Kenny, "The good ol' days of Las Vegas."

CHAPEL OF THE FLOWERS

1717 S. LAS VEGAS BLVD. • LAS VEGAS, NV 89104

(702) 735-4331 • LITTLECHAPEL.COM

A Not-So-Vegas Wedding

*I*f you want to get married in Las Vegas, there are 192 wedding chapels from which you can choose. Only in Las Vegas can you get married while still seated comfortably in your own car or by an Elvis lookalike who, after he pronounces you man and wife, serenades you with "Love Me Tender." Las Vegas is probably the only place in the world where you can invite Brad and Angelina to your wedding and they have to come. Certainly it is the only place where you can get married with sharks, ghouls, or goblins as your witnesses. In Vegas you can get married at the top of the Eiffel Tower, in the gardens of Venus, in a gondola on Venetian waters, underwater in an aquarium, in a neon boneyard, or at a downtown Denny's.

With so many venues to choose from, it's easy to see how close to 130,000 weddings are performed here each year. It's also difficult to know just which venue to choose. There is one place in Las Vegas, however, that allows you to combine history with elegance. The Chapel of the Flowers has been a Las Vegas landmark for close to sixty years. The chapel got its start when Thomas G. Myers purchased the property in the 1950s and leased it out for thirty years to a man who built a tiny wedding chapel right next to the Strip. The man leased the entire property from Thomas, subleasing the part he wasn't using to a car salesman and an auto shop. When the thirty-year lease was up in 1989, Thomas and his two sons decided to go into the wedding business for themselves. They tore down the chapel and turned the entire property into a wedding venue. They also changed the name of the chapel. "We dropped the 'little,' because we weren't so little anymore," says director of operations Nicole Robertson.

Instead of falling into the typical Vegas kitsch, Thomas and his sons decided to build a venue where people could have an elegant wedding without paying the high costs typically associated with a casino-venue wedding. A wedding at the Chapel of the Flowers is "a non-Vegas wedding in Las Vegas," says Thomas's son Jason. "We focus on the true seriousness and excitement of your wedding, unlike the reputation Vegas sometimes has of quickie weddings."

Instead of worrying about how many weddings they perform each year—or each day for that matter—the chapel chooses instead to make sure every couple has the best wedding experience possible. At the Chapel of the Flowers, you'll never feel rushed. Getting you in and out before the next couple arrives is not their thing. They're more about making sure the entire wedding experience is personalized to the bride and groom, which is why they perform no more than three weddings at a time at the chapel venue.

The chapel's wedding packages can take care of more than just the wedding day. They can arrange a special post-wedding dinner or a honeymoon villa for your wedding night. They can transport you to and from the chapel, even in separate bride and groom limos so the groom doesn't see the bride before the wedding. They can take care of all the flowers at their in-house floral shop, do the bride's hair and make-up, and provide the wedding dress, bridesmaid dresses, and/or tuxes. They even have someone who can play live organ music at your ceremony. The chapel has photographers who can take all the photos—both on- and off-site—and even have those photos transferred to albums or canvas. "We're known for the quality of our photography," says Nicole. The chapel can provide both traditional photos and the "documentary-style" photos that "tell the fairy tale of your wedding."

If you prefer not to get married at any of the chapel's five wedding venues, they can arrange for you to marry on a yacht, on the floor of the Grand Canyon, or in the Valley of Fire. They can even arrange for a ceremony at the iconic WELCOME TO LAS VEGAS sign. The Chapel of the Flowers truly specializes in catering to a couple's every need.

Couples who do choose to marry at the Chapel of the Flowers have three indoor chapels—La Cappella, the Victorian chapel, and the

Magnolia chapel—and two outdoor venues—a gazebo and a garden—to choose from. One of those outdoor venues is the Glass Garden, an area closed off by large, decorative gates. Although you are in the heart of downtown Las Vegas, this location gives the illusion of being in a beautiful outdoor garden. Molded rocks provide the backdrop to the bride and groom and the entire area is decorated with hundreds of brightly colored glass flowers, which give the venue its name. Guests sit in white folding chairs and the entire ceremony is performed outside.

While they appreciate their history in Las Vegas, the owners are constantly looking for ways to beautify the venue. "We work to continually upgrade the beautiful chapels and grounds to ensure each bride and groom get their ideal wedding venue as well as stunning backdrops for the perfect wedding photos," Jason says. The attention to detail seems to be working. The Chapel of the Flowers was named one of the Top 10 Unique Vegas Weddings by *MSN Travel*. It was also inducted into the Best of Weddings Hall of Fame by *TheKnot .com* and won the Bride's Choice Awards for Best Wedding Venue from *WeddingWire.com*. The chapel also won Best Wedding Chapel by the readers of the *Las Vegas Review Journal* and their website was named Best Website by both the *Las Vegas Wedding Awards* and *Beautiful Bride* (magazine).

The Chapel of the Flowers is unique in Las Vegas not just because of its history, but its concentration on the bride and groom. One of the favorite traditions of the Chapel of the Flowers is the red chair. The red velvet chair, which sits outside adjacent to the gazebo, was purchased simply to provide a place to sit. Since then it has become the subject of must-have photos. "Everyone wants a picture sitting on the chair," says Nicole. "They ask for it specifically."

CHICAGO JOE'S

820 S. 4TH ST. • LAS VEGAS, NV 89101

(702) 382-5637 • CHICAGOJOESRESTAURANT.COM

Now That's a Meatball

It's like being in your mother's or grandmother's house," says Joe Collura, the "Joe" of Chicago Joe's, explaining why his family opened their restaurant in an intimate brick house built in 1933. "Being in a house, you reminisce," says Joe. "You think about family and you feel at home." Opening the Italian restaurant in a house was actually his mother's idea. The family bought the house in 1974, took four months to convert it into a restaurant, and opened Chicago Joe's in 1975. Apparently it was a good idea because the restaurant has been in the same location for more than four decades.

Family is important to Joe and it is because of that family that Joe is even in the restaurant business. He was born in Chicago, on Halloween, and it was in the windy city that his grandmother—Maria Penacchio—opened her first restaurant, a pizzeria she named Nino. The restaurant, which opened in 1952, was a success; one that led to the family opening a banquet hall and then adding a fine-dining restaurant onto the pizzeria. It was in that restaurant that Joe got his first real taste of the family business, working as a dishwasher alongside his father and uncle—both of whom were named Joe. "On Saturday nights we had four Joes," explains Joe. "My dad was 'Big Joe,' my uncle was 'Little Joe,' and I was 'Joey.' There was also an employee named Joe. We called him 'Mustache Joe' because he had a mustache."

Of course the man who would eventually lose the moniker "Joey" wasn't the only Chicago Joe. "The first Chicago Joe was my uncle," he explains, and it was that Joe—Little Joe—who suggested the family

move to Las Vegas after the death of Big Joe in 1971. Joe didn't buy into his uncle's idea and wasn't thrilled about the thought of moving. But his mother asked him to try it out for a year, so he made the move. Now he loves Las Vegas and can't imagine living anywhere else. However, even though he's moved to a completely different town, he's still surrounded by Joes. "We've got three Joes working here now. I'm Joe. There's also 'J.' and 'J.R.,'" explains Joe.

Chicago Joe's was a hit from the day it opened, so much so that in 1980 Las Vegas icon and mob front man Moe Dalitz approached Little Joe and asked him to open a second Chicago Joe's in the Sundance Hotel and Casino on the Las Vegas Strip. Moe Dalitz wasn't the type of man you said no to, so a second Chicago Joe's was opened inside the casino, where it remained for ten years. In fact, the only reason the restaurant closed was because the new owner, who was changing the name of the hotel and casino to the Fitzgerald's, did not renew the lease.

After Little Joe's death, Joe and his sister inherited the restaurant, with Joe running its operations. At the same time, Little Joe's wife Joan opened Chicago Joe's Hideaway at the Silk Purse Ranch on the outskirts of Las Vegas. Joan ran the restaurant for nearly five years before she had to close the doors. Through it all the original

Vintage Spot
LUV-IT FROZEN CUSTARD: EST. 1973

The little blue building has been serving some of the most delicious custard on earth for more than forty years. They are best known for serving interesting flavors like chocolate pretzel, rum rainbow, banana nut, root beer float, and death by chocolate. Luv-It attracts locals, tourists, lawyers, artists, families, and even celebrities—though those people tend to give their orders through black-tinted windows.
505 E. Oakey Blvd.; (702) 384-6452; luvitfrozencustard.com

Chicago Joe's has remained open even when a decision by the city of Las Vegas to make Fourth Street a one-way street almost killed his business. The project took eighteen months to complete and during that time people, wanting to avoid the construction, stopped coming in as regularly. "It took five and a half years to build the business back," says Joe, but build it they did.

Family is still just as important as ever to Joe. Having been trained by his mother, Joe's wife Marlene has been running the kitchen for the last twenty-five years. "I couldn't do it without her," says Joe with a broad smile. "My wife's got a heart of gold. When she comes out of the kitchen, she gets hugs from everybody." In many ways Chicago Joe's is the same restaurant the family opened in 1975, but in some ways it has changed. While most of the recipes are the ones passed down from Joe's grandmother—"About 80 percent," says Joe—some items, such as tripe (stomach) have been removed from the menu. And, of course, Joe is always looking to update and improve the menu whenever possible, which is how he and his mother came up with one of their most famous recipes—cioppino, or seafood stew.

Many items on the menu are Chicago Joe's staples. "The stuffed artichoke is really popular," says Joe. So too are the lasagna, veal and peppers, and the traditional spaghetti and meatballs, which, by the way, is how you judge a good Italian restaurant—by their meatballs. Joe's are a mix of beef and pork and, most importantly, taste just like a homemade meatball should. And the sauce . . . oh, the sauce. "Our sauce is Sicilian," explains Joe. "It's a deeper red and a little on the sweet side."

Chicago Joe's isn't fancy, but you wouldn't want it to be. The main dining room only seats around twenty-four, but there is more seating in the back room. The tables are covered with plastic red-and-white picnic-style tablecloths, padded wood captain's chairs serve as seats, and big band–era music plays throughout the restaurant. The floor is wood and white lace curtains hang over every window. If you were raised Italian you'll feel right at home, but don't worry, even if you weren't you'll fit right in. "I still smile, shake hands, and love the people," says Joe. It is a clientele that is loyal and growing. "I can't tell you how many customers have been here from the beginning," he says. "I have people who tell me, 'I used to come in here when I was this big and now I come in with my kids.'" It's something that makes Joe very happy. "We're on the next generation," he says with a proud smile—and why shouldn't he be?

THE CLARK COUNTY MUSEUM

1830 S. BOULDER HWY. • HENDERSON, NV 89002

(702) 455-7955 • CLARKCOUNTYNV.GOV

Take a Walk Down Heritage Street

In Las Vegas the word "vintage" usually refers to something from the 1950s or 1960s. It usually has something to do with the Rat Pack, Elvis, the Mob or anything from that era. However, at the Clark County Museum, the word "vintage" takes on a whole new meaning. At this museum, "vintage" goes back just a little farther than the '50s or '60s, long before casinos, the likes of Bugsy Siegel, or an imposing cement structure built to tame a raging river. "Vintage" refers to a time when the Paiute Indians roamed the land; a time when explorers like John Charles Frémont, John Wesley Powell, and Jedediah Smith first came into the valley and found it both alluring and deadly.

"We tell the story of what it was like to live here—why people settled here in the first place," says Mark P. Hall-Patten, administrator for the Clark County Museum. "Our focus is on the history of southern Nevada. There are good reasons we are here and we tell that story." Mark sits at a desk piled high with books, clippings, historical records, and memorabilia. If you've watched an episode of the History Channel's *Pawn Stars* in the last decade, you've probably seen Mark. He's the one with the two-tone beard and flat brimmed Atwood hat, usually wearing a red shirt—and no, he's not Amish. While *Pawn Stars* keeps him busy, it isn't his main gig. Mark is the administrator of three museums, two in Las Vegas and one in nearby Searchlight, Nevada. Mark, who graduated from the University of Delaware, knows more about history than anyone on this planet. Okay, that might be a stretch, but he does know quite a bit and all you have to do is spend even a small amount of time with him to find out just what he knows. Mark's interest in museums started at a very young age. "I used to build museums on my patio when I was eight," he says. Once his museum was built—typically with items he found in his house— he'd force his siblings to take the tour that he would host. "They hated it," Mark says, but the experience laid the groundwork for his entire future.

One of the things people always complain about in Las Vegas is that we have no culture. The people who say that just don't know where to find it. And it's a good bet none of those people have ever been to the Clark County Museum. Here you can find a flintlock musket from around 1840, candle molds from the 1850s, and mining equipment from the 1870s. You can also learn about early Las Vegas settlers such as Octavius Decatur Gass who, after a failed mining venture in 1865, took over the abandoned Mormon Fort and turned it into a ranch and way station for weary travelers. Gass ran the ranch until 1880 when he lost the property to Archibald Stewart, who had loaned Gass five thousand dollars. When Gass was unable to pay, Stewart took over the ranch. Archibald's wife Helen J. Stewart would eventually sell a portion of the ranch—after her husband's untimely death at the hand of Schuyler Henry—to William Andrews Clark and J. Ross Clark. In 1905 the two brothers auctioned off the land in parcels, creating the City of Las Vegas.

The Clark County Museum is probably the only place where you can find the cowboy boots belonging to longtime Las Vegas constable W. W. "Woody" Cole, alongside a photo of Cole posing with comedians Bud Abbott and Lou Costello. It's also likely the only place where you can find one of the .30 caliber Browning machine guns used at the Las Vegas Gunnery School, right below the July 13, 1942, edition of *Time* magazine showing a member of that school holding the machine gun on its cover. The museum also has a remnant of a still used in Prohibition times, a section of cable from the Hoover Dam, and goggles meant to protect the wearer's eyes from an atomic flash. If Las Vegas culture to you means Elvis, you're in luck because the museum has an Elvis Presley doll dressed in the famous jumpsuit and cape he wore while performing at the Las Vegas Hilton.

The museum got its start in 1968 when Anna Roberts Parks donated several items to the city of Henderson, Nevada, with the

thought of creating a museum. Parks was the founder of Palm Mortuary, which itself has been in the valley since 1926. "She had several items in her personal collection, including a stuffed penguin," says Mark, adding, "We still have the penguin." A nonprofit organization was formed and the items were used to open the Southern Nevada Museum in the gymnasium of a local school that has since been torn down. In 1974 the City of Henderson donated the thirty acres of land on which the museum currently sits. "There was nothing out here at that time," explains Mark. "Not a building, not even a road."

Shortly after the museum acquired the land, the Union Pacific Railroad contacted them, looking to donate the train depot they had once used in Boulder City to a nonprofit organization. "At that point we weren't really sure what we were going to be as a museum," says Mark. But when someone offers you a building, you take it—and take it they did. The depot became the first building to be placed on the property. In 1979 Clark County Commissioner Robert Broadbent pushed the county to take over the museum. His push was successful and the Southern Nevada Museum became the Clark County Heritage Museum, and later the Clark County Museum. That same year two other significant occurrences happened at the museum.

The items in the gymnasium museum were moved to the thirty-five-acre property because the school had been condemned. In addition, the Beckley family was looking to donate their family home, a California-style bungalow, which was located on Fourth Street in downtown Las Vegas. The house, which was built in 1912 at a cost of $2,500, came with all its furnishings. Now with the depot and the Beckley house, the museum started heading in a distinct direction. As buildings were donated, they were placed on opposite sides of a street, which the museum named Heritage Street.

Heritage Street is now home to five houses, a print shop, and a silver Spartanette travel trailer with a motor court cabin. A small, but elegant, wedding chapel—the Candlelight Wedding Chapel—is located to the rear of the Babcock and Wilcox House, just east of the Museum Guild Gazebo. All of the houses are on the *Directory of Historic House Museums* in the United States. Each is decorated in the theme of a different time period and each has been made to look as if it was built in its current location, complete with manicured lawns and developed trees. In fact Heritage Street could look like any street in hometown America.

In 1990 the main museum building was constructed and it is in this building that many of the exhibits are housed. Here you will find, as you might expect, an exhibit dedicated to gambling. In this exhibit there is a 1989 Dewey slot machine, named for Spanish-American War hero Admiral George Dewey. There is even a side profile image of Dewey molded into the slot machine. While the machine bore his name, Dewey may not have been pleased with this honor. That's because the slot machine could be rigged by dishonest casino operators to prevent certain colors from landing on the pay line. If you chose that color, you'd never win, no matter how much money you spent.

The museum also has a 1910 Mills slot machine that paid its winnings in gum, a 1965 automatic "21" machine that used a real deck of cards, and a 1935 Mills Castle Front slot machine. There is even a penny machine from the long-ago-demolished Mint. You can play the machine, but it won't pay out. In typical Las Vegas odds, all the money put in the slot machine gets donated to the museum.

In a world where museum attendance can come with a high price tag, the Clark County Museum keeps its fees low—so low, in fact, that

Vintage Spot

THE HOWARD W. CANNON AVIATION MUSEUM: EST. 1993

If you've ever walked through McCarran Airport you've probably been to the Howard W. Cannon Aviation Museum and didn't even realize it. Instead of placing the museum in a room off to the side, Mark P. Hall-Patten, administrator for the Howard W. Cannon Aviation Museum, chose to place it out in the open where it is easily seen and accessible. You can find a plane hanging from the ceiling or a mint red T-Bird in exhibits that stretch throughout the airport into every terminal. This museum also has the distinction of being the only one of its kind funded by the airport in which it's located.

5757 Wayne Newton Blvd.; (702) 261-5211; mccarran.com

they hardly seem real. Adult admission is a mere two dollars, while children and seniors get in for a single dollar. Mark, who has often been criticized for charging so little, has a very good reason for where he sets the fees. "I don't ever want a family to be turned away from the gates because they can't afford it," he says. And that, my friends, makes this museum the best bet in town.

DI BELLA FLOWERS AND GIFTS

2021 W. CHARLESTON BLVD. • LAS VEGAS, NV 89102

(702) 384-1121 • DIBELLAFLOWERS.COM

Desert Rose

John and Sue Di Bella have certainly seen a lot in their thirty years of business in Las Vegas. When you open a flower shop in the wedding capital of the world and you position that shop across from one of the oldest hospitals in Las Vegas, you're bound to have a story or two, or three . . . or several hundred. "We've seen quite a bit," John says with a sly smile that gives you the sense he's seen more than he's willing to tell. "We were the official flower shop for the Summa Corporation," John explains, "which means we delivered flowers to many of the stars." Those stars include such notables as Frank Sinatra, Sammy Davis Jr., Wayne Newton, Robert Goulet, and Phyllis McGuire of the famous McGuire Sisters.

John and Sue opened their flower shop in 1984, but John's love for flowers dates back well into his youth. "I was always a gardener," says John, whose family moved to Las Vegas in 1962. And with a name like Di Bella—"Bella" being Italian for beautiful—a destiny with flowers seems inevitable. While still in his teens John found he had a bit of a knack for arranging those flowers. "I made a couple of cor-sages in high school and people started asking me to make theirs." He did, selling those corsages to his fellow classmates. While in high school John took a job at Dover's Flowers, which was on the corner of Las Vegas Boulevard and Fremont Street, as a delivery driver. "I didn't really know what I was doing," John said, which is probably why he only had the job for six months.

Undaunted, John got another job at a flower shop, this time at Ruby's Flowers, which was located on Las Vegas Boulevard just south

of Main. It was while working at Ruby's that he both learned the art of floral design and made a decision that would affect the rest of his life. John decided to attend a college in Wisconsin called Gateway Technical Institute, which specialized in the floral business. While going to Gateway, John took a job at a floral shop owned by Louise Turner—a founding member of FTD. Louise had a daughter named Sue and when John saw her working in the corner arranging flowers, Cupid's arrow struck. "She was so beautiful," says John with a bright smile, quickly adding, "Well, she still is."

John and Sue began a relationship and when college ended, Sue moved to Las Vegas with John. The two got jobs at Patio Flowers and it was while working there that the couple took an afternoon off to get married. "It was just her and I," John said of their wedding. "Sue made her veil and I made the flowers." The couple married in the Little Chapel of the West—another Las Vegas icon—and have been married for forty-three years.

John and Sue worked at several flower shops, eventually landing at Palm Mortuary in their shop called Flowers by Palm—which consisted of two rooms and a refrigerator. They worked there for eight years, before deciding a change was in order. In 1984 John and Sue decided to go out on their own. John's friend—a real estate agent—showed him several properties, but John and Sue didn't really have the money to pay for a commercial building. Then they found a house across the street from the University Medical Center—which was, ironically, where John's mother worked as a nurse for twenty-five years.

"The house wasn't for sale," explains John, but that didn't stop his friend from approaching the owner anyway. He and John knocked on the door and were allowed inside. Even after he saw the home, John wasn't convinced, but his friend talked him into buying it. "The house turned out to be a blessing in disguise," says John. "Because it was a home, we were able to get a regular home mortgage. We probably wouldn't have been able to get a commercial loan."

John put his money down and afterward he had seven thousand dollars left for opening inventory. All that was left was the visit from the inspector so the house could be rezoned for commercial use. "The inspector told us the place had to be updated," explains John. And the cost for the updates? You guessed it, seven thousand dollars. John and Sue paid what was needed and managed to scrape together enough money for inventory and the rest, as they say, is history.

Di Bella's has been a Las Vegas staple in the flower industry for many years and they have a loyal following. People who have bought flowers at Di Bella's now have kids who buy flowers at Di Bella's. This is because John, Sue, and their staff do whatever is needed to make sure their customers are happy. When a client's wedding venue was changed eight hours before their ceremony, John himself transported the flowers to the new location and made sure the setup was perfect for the bride and groom's special day. "It looked like someone had been planning the setup for weeks," said the bride when it was all over.

Walking into Di Bella Flowers and Gifts is like walking into the best-smelling garden in the world. But then again, it is filled with flowers of all types, colors, and sizes. Whether you want gladiolus, carnations, daisies, roses, or sunflowers you can get them at Di Bella's. If you want snapdragons, lilies, orchids, daffodils, or birds of paradise, you can get those too and many more, because John and Sue are one of the few florists in Las Vegas who have their own greenhouse on location. Besides flowers, you can get all your floral necessities at

Di Bella's. They have everything from cards to vases. They even have stuffed animals—a perfect flower companion.

Over the years John and Sue have made many friends, but none more famous than Joan Rivers. "She knows her flowers," says John. "She likes flowers that have a fragrance to them." Probably because most Las Vegas dressing rooms were located next to smelly kitchens, or worse. Through the many years of delivering flowers to Joan's dressing rooms, a friendship was struck. "When she was in town she'd invite us to her show," says John. "Of all the stars we delivered flowers to, Joan was the only one who always sent a thank-you."

The reason for John's and Sue's success is not only their knowledge of flowers or their skill in arranging those flowers, it's also their customer service. The Di Bellas pride themselves on treating the customer the way they'd want to be treated themselves. Whether you're in the shop or on the phone, you truly feel like you're their only customer. That's because right then and there, you are.

DOÑA MARIA TAMALES RESTAURANT

910 S. LAS VEGAS BLVD. • LAS VEGAS, NV 89101
(702) 382-6538 • DONAMARIATAMALES.COM

Chili Today, Hot Tamale

The landscape of downtown Las Vegas is rapidly changing. It seems that a new restaurant, business, or destination opens almost daily. Old buildings are being either revamped and refurbished or torn down to make way for the new. It's exciting and a little unsettling. As the "new" moves into the "old," many vintage places are simply disappearing, but not all of them. Some, like Doña Maria Tamales Restaurant, are more than holding steady in downtown Las Vegas; they're thriving.

Positioned right on Las Vegas Boulevard is an unassuming little Mexican restaurant that looks exactly like what you'd expect a Mexican restaurant to look like—on the inside anyway. This is apparent the moment you walk through the glass rose-embossed doors. The floor is covered with earth-tone Mexican tile. The walls have a pinkish-orange tint and, as you'd expect, are decorated with traditional Mexican artifacts, such as sombreros, Aztec calendars, and brightly painted sun faces made of fired clay. Covering almost every wall are murals depicting traditional Mexican scenes. On one wall women are busy grinding corn into meal by hand. On another, a young girl is picking sunflowers in a meadow at the base of a mountain. Still another shows a scene from a village celebration complete with colorful banners. A wall at the front of the restaurant celebrates Mexico's rich boxing heritage. Positioned on this wall are two pugilists posing before an impending match. Boxing posters of all the greats hang on the wall on either side of the mural. There is even a pair of signed gloves.

Once you've devoured the scenery, you can get down to the reason you came here in the first place—the food. You're barely seated before a basket of homemade tortilla chips and salsa arrive at your table. The chips are a particular treat and it's easy to fill up on them before the meal even arrives. If you can stop munching on chips long enough to look at the menu, you'll find a vast array of traditional Mexican favorites, like burritos, enchiladas, tacos, tostadas, and, of course, tamales—the item for which the restaurant is famous. They have pork, chicken, beef, or cheese. They even have dessert tamales with pineapple and raisins. You can order them from the menu in singles or pairs and if you want to take a bunch of them home, you can get a dozen or half dozen.

Vintage Spots

RICARDO'S: EST. 1979

This family-owned restaurant has been serving tacos, enchiladas, burritos, tamales, and quesadillas for over forty years. As it expanded through the Las Vegas valley, it actually sold its Flamingo location before reacquiring and revamping it several years later. The family has now concentrated their efforts solely on the Flamingo location, which is open twenty-four hours.

4930 W. Flamingo Rd.; (702) 227-9100; recardosoflasvegas.com

MACAYO'S MEXICAN KITCHEN: EST. 1959

While this Mexican restaurant opened in 1959, its roots go back to 1946 when Woody and Victoria Johnson opened their first Macayo's in Phoenix, Arizona. The couple would eventually open fourteen locations in Arizona and three in Las Vegas, with the Charleston location being the oldest. The company is now in the capable hands of their children—Sharisse, Gary, and Stephen.

1741 E. Charleston Blvd.; (702) 382-5605; macayo.com

Doña Maria Tamales Restaurant got its start in 1979 as a small to-go restaurant on the corner of 10th Street and Charleston in a shopping center. When it opened it was run by an ex-soccer player by the name of Alfredo Martinez. "My dad played soccer and my mother was a cheerleader," says Neriza Johnson, Doña Maria's current owner. As Neriza tells it, Alfredo noticed a young woman by the name of Elvia cheering on the sidelines, so he went over and introduced himself. "It was love at first sight," she says. The two married after only three months and forty-two years later they're still going strong.

After soccer ended, Alfredo took up construction, which eventually brought the couple from California to Las Vegas. Using his grandmother's recipe, Alfredo began cooking tamales and selling them out of their small Charleston restaurant. The tamales were a hit. "That's what put them on the map," says Neriza. "They're still the most popular item on the menu." At first Alfredo did most of the cooking. "My mom didn't know how to cook when they got married, so my dad showed her," says Neriza, who quickly adds, "Now she's a great cook."

Neriza herself is something of an anomaly, a Las Vegas native, born and raised. Even from a young age, she was destined to follow her parent's footsteps into the family business. "I had to work there at lunchtime when I was little," she explains, "It was a great experience."

One that allowed her to take the reins when her parents were ready to retire. "I love the restaurant business," she says. "It's a lot of long hours, but it's also very rewarding."

In 1990 Alfredo and Elvia outgrew their little place in the shopping center. A short distance away was a building on Las Vegas Boulevard that used to be Antonio's Italian Restaurant. They bought it, remodeled it, and were back in business, only now they were selling more than just their famous tamales. Along with the traditional menu, Doña Maria also serves breakfast Mexican-style with huevos a la Mexicana, huevos con chile verde, and huevos rancheros. If you prefer, they also serve an American breakfast, complete with two eggs, pancakes, and a side of ham or bacon.

Eight years after they opened on the Strip, they expanded to a place across town. Now there are two Doña Maria Tamales Restaurants, each serving the same Mexican fare. And it's not only the customers that are loyal to Doña Maria, it's the employees as well. "We have employees that have been with us for twenty-five years," says Neriza, who understands that no success can be achieved alone. "You have to surround yourself with good people," she says. "We have to depend on each other." Neriza shares the same view as did her parents when it comes to the people she works with. "We're family," she says. After serving the community for over thirty-five years, Doña Maria Tamales Restaurant shows no signs of letting up. In 2010 they were listed by *Zagat* as one of the Area's Top Restaurants. Hot today and tamale.

EL CORTEZ HOTEL & CASINO

600 E. FREMONT ST. • LAS VEGAS, NV 89101
(702) 385-5200 • ELCORTEZHOTELCASINO.COM

Looking Ahead to the Past

*Y*ou can't help but get a sense of history when you walk in," says Alexandra Epstein, executive vice president of the El Cortez Hotel & Casino. It's clear to see that Alexandra, who goes by Alex, is proud of the hotel her family owns—proud of its past and of her family's commitment to keep that past alive. "You don't find many Las Vegas properties that give you a sense of history, but El Cortez is one of them." That history is easy to see even before you walk through the doors of the oldest continually operating hotel and casino in Las Vegas.

The El Cortez got its start in 1941 when John Kell Houssels joined with John Grayson and Marion Hicks to build the Spanish Ranch–style hotel and casino at a cost of $245,000. Houssels, who had trained as a biplane pilot during World War I, had moved his family to Las Vegas in 1929 after working as an assayer in both Nevada and California. Houssels' training may have been as an assayer, but his interests lay in gambling. Before long he had purchased one-third interest in a downtown poker room called the Smokehouse. In 1931 when gambling was legalized in the state of Nevada, Houssels applied for and was granted a gambling license. He renamed the Smokehouse the Las Vegas Club and revitalized the place, taking it from a gambling parlor and turning it into a small casino. In 1941 he set his sights on another property a little farther downtown.

When it opened, the El Cortez had fifty-nine rooms and was the first resort-style hotel in downtown Las Vegas. The resort was built so far from the other downtown casinos—two whole blocks—that

many worried the property would never be successful. In fact, several people jokingly referred to it as being "out in the country." Their worries would prove to be unfounded, for in only four short years the property had done so well that it attracted the attention of a Midwest group whose members included mobsters Moe Sedway, Meyer Lansky, and Benjamin "Bugsy" Siegel. Houssels sold the property to the group in 1945 for $600,000.

Siegel ran the horse book in the El Cortez, but his interests weren't only in that property. Siegel had been sent to Las Vegas by Meyer Lansky and Charles "Lucky" Luciano to take over the race and sports book betting in Las Vegas. Siegel carried out his directive and by the time the El Cortez was sold to the organization of which he was a part, Siegel had managed to take control of 50 percent of every horse book in downtown Las Vegas and 33 percent of both the El Rancho and the Last Frontier, which were located on Highway 91 just outside of town.

Unfortunately, owning a casino and running a casino proved to be two different things and despite a major interior remodeling, the Midwest group were having trouble running the place. So a year after they bought it, they contacted Houssels and asked him to come back. In 1946 Houssels got with Utah-based Ray Salmon and leased the casino back from its organized crime-rooted owners. Even though the interior had been remodeled only a year earlier, Houssels put $250,000 into expanding the El Cortez, adding a barbershop, a nightclub, a swimming pool, and a four-story wing. That same year Houssels took full ownership of the Las Vegas Club and sold property he had earlier acquired on Highway 91—later called the Las Vegas Strip—to Marion Hicks, his former partner. Hicks would use the spot to build the Thunderbird Hotel and Casino in 1948.

However, gambling wasn't the only thing that piqued Houssels' interests. He also owned a bus company, a taxicab company, a popular restaurant in downtown Las Vegas called the Round-Up, and the Overland Hotel, and he was an avid thoroughbred horse racer. Houssels, who was the president of the Nevada Racing Association, even once won the Santa Anita Derby with his horse Bymeabond in 1945.

In 1952 the property received yet another facelift—again only on the interior. The bar inside the casino was renamed the Buccaneer Bar and the cocktail waitresses were dressed up as pirates. The hotel's supper club would eventually fall victim to the pirate life as well, being renamed the Pirate's Den in 1953. The pirate theme became so popular that the casino began using pirate graphics in its advertising. The Pirate's Den would have the distinction of hiring Pat Gallagher, who, at the time, was the only female maître d' in Las Vegas. While the El Cortez continued in its popularity, alas, the pirate theme did not and by 1957 it was abandoned altogether.

In 1952 the hotel also installed what would become one of downtown Las Vegas's most famous landmarks—a roof-mounted sign. "The sign is one of our most valuable assets," says Alex, referring to the beacon that still sits atop the property. It consists of a metal framework on which are mounted the words EL CORTEZ written in italics and HOTEL written in capital block letters. Below the block letters are the words COFFEE SHOP & BAR and under those are the words FREE PARKING. All the words are outlined with neon and when the sign lights up at night, it can't help but steal your attention from whatever else you may be looking at.

In 1963 Houssels sold the El Cortez for $4.6 million to a man who would become a Las Vegas icon—Jackie Gaughan. John Davis "Jackie" Gaughan Jr. first came to Las Vegas while serving in the military at

Vintage Spots

EL CORTEZ CABANA SUITES: EST. 2008

In 2008 the El Cortez bought out the Ogden Hotel right across the street. The sixty-four-room property was turned into a boutique hotel, combining modern conveniences with vintage Vegas style. While the hotel may have been updated, the building itself dates back to 1975.

651 E. Ogden Ave.; (702) 385-5200

LA COMIDA: EST. 2013

While this Mexican restaurant only opened in 2013, what makes the place vintage is the building itself. The La Comida is positioned in the building that once housed the laundry facilities for the El Cortez. The decor features mismatched furniture, old-fashioned light fixtures, and windows that allow the entire front of the place to open to the outside. It also has what is probably the coolest sign in the history of signs—a neon-infused seven-foot-tall Day of the Dead monkey that climbs the outside of the building.

100 Sixth St.; (702) 463-9900; lacomidalv.com

JERRY'S NUGGET: EST. 1964

This family-owned casino, which is a locals' favorite, has been serving Las Vegas for fifty years. Started by two Jer-rys—Jerry Lodge and Jerry Stamis—the Nugget rests on the site that was once the Town House Bar. While the hotel and casino fell into bankruptcy in 2013, it recovered in only eight months and, having made significant improvements to the property, Jerry's Nugget is still going strong.

1821 N. Las Vegas Blvd.; (702) 399-3000; jerrysnugget.com

Nellis Air Force Base. The son of an Omaha bookmaker, Gaughan would eventually own interests in eight downtown Las Vegas casinos. Under Gaughan's direction, the El Cortez continued to prosper and became a locals' favorite. In 1980 he added a tower to the property, bringing the total room count to 297.

While Gaughan would eventually sell all his other properties, he held on to his beloved El Cortez, even living on the top floor of the hotel. However, in 2008, at the age of eighty-seven, Gaughan sold the hotel to Ike Gaming, leaving the property he loved in the very capable hands of Kenny Epstein, who had worked with Gaughan since 1975. Epstein and his family have a unique way of looking at the property. "We're going to continue to evolve," says Alex. "We want to strike a balance between that old Las Vegas experience and that new tech-savvy customer moving downtown." It would seem that the Epsteins know exactly how to do just that. Except for the tower Gaughan added in 1980, the outside of the El Cortez looks much the same as it did when it was built originally. And walking inside you get the feeling you've entered a casino that looks just like it may have looked back in 1941. The ceilings are low, just as they were originally when pit bosses used to walk catwalks above the players to make sure no one was cheating. However, the mirrored ceilings have been replaced with acoustic ceiling tiles and elegant light fixtures.

The interior of the casino, which was placed on the National Register of Historic Places in 2013, is decorated in rich dark wood and there are photos of old Las Vegas mounted on almost every wall. Unlike most casinos, the El Cortez manages to look both vintage and modern at the same time. "People love it," says Alex. "We all have this nostalgia for vintage Las Vegas." While the El Cortez has changed hands, this doesn't seem to have affected its popularity. "It's a family on all sides," explains Alex. "We have customers who have been coming for decades. We also have employees who have been working here for decades. We're a family." It's a family that both honors its past and is excited by its future possibilities. "We love Las Vegas and downtown," says Alex. "Looking ahead we're excited to be part of the future."

ETHEL M CHOCOLATES

2 CACTUS GARDEN DR. • HENDERSON, NV 89014

(702) 435-2608 • ETHELM.COM

A Hidden Chocolaty Gem

Vegas often bills itself as a hedonistic playground. Our official slogan even encourages that view: "What Happens Here Stays Here." Tourists who come to Las Vegas expect to find just about everything they could ever want in their pursuit of pleasure. As a town, we typically live up to those expectations. Here tourists can find exotic drinks, fine dining, unique entertainment, and, of course, chocolate. Really? Chocolate in the desert? But, you may wisely ask, doesn't chocolate melt in the desert? Of course it does, but if you're looking to satisfy your self-indulgent desires, you can't possibly leave out chocolate. And in Vegas, they haven't.

While alcohol, food, and entertainment are all readily available, to find a factory dedicated to making chocolate the old-fashioned way—in small batches, with no preservatives—you have to get off the strip and take a little trip to the southeast part of the valley to find Ethel M Chocolates. While the Ethel M Chocolate Factory has only been in business since 1981, its roots go back well over one hundred years. That is because the "M" in Ethel M stands for a well-known and respected brand of chocolates, one that is responsible for such favorites as M&M, Snickers, Milky Way, Dove, and, of course, its namesake, the Mars bar.

Mars Incorporated got its start in 1911, when Frank C. Mars opened the Mars Candy Factory in Tacoma, Washington. Frank, who had polio as a child, learned how to hand-dip chocolate from his mother Alva in their Hancock, Minnesota, kitchen. He used those techniques to make the buttercream candy that he sold out of his own kitchen in

Washington. In 1920 Frank moved his business to a larger facility in Minneapolis. Three years later the Milky Way bar was introduced and billed as "chocolate malted milk in a candy bar." The bar was a huge success and launched the company that would become Mars Incorporated. In 1929, the business was again moved, this time to Chicago, and it was there that Forrest Edward Mars—son of Frank and his first wife Ethel G. Kissack—entered the family business. With the success of the Milky Way bar, the company added hit after hit with Snickers in 1930 and The 3 Musketeers in 1932.

In 1932 Forrest moved to the United Kingdom, where he created the Mars bar, which was mass-produced for UK troops. In 1940 Forrest returned to the United States and established M&M Limited in Newark, New Jersey. After running the business for over thirty years, Forrest officially retired in 1969; however, when chocolate is part of your DNA, retiring doesn't always stick. Such was the case with Forrest Mars, who had a desire to go back to the old ways, to making chocolates in the kitchen, just like his mother Ethel had taught him to do. So he moved to Henderson, Nevada, and opened Ethel M Chocolates, naming the business after his mother—Ethel Mars.

Ethel M Chocolates is a tribute to Ethel Mars and the techniques she taught Forrest as a child. In fact, the majority of the gourmet chocolates are made from Ethel's own recipes. Ethel M Chocolates isn't like every other chocolate factory. Here you won't find thousands of one type of candy bar made every day. "We do small batches because we don't use preservatives," says packaging buyer Lindsay Wold, who herself started at the factory as a tour guide. Another thing that makes Ethel M different is that you can actually watch the chocolates being made. "We do as much as we can by hand," says Lindsay.

This is evident with a walk down the viewing aisle, which is a type of self-guided tour that not only affords a view of the factory floor, but also has videos and photos showing the history of the factory and the grounds on which the factory sits. Here you can see workers lifting kettles of hot pecan brittle, an Ethel M signature item, and pouring it onto large tables where it is shaped and, once it is cooled, cut. Through the viewing windows you can also find workers hand-dipping strawberries into chocolate, coating apples, or, just like Lucy did, checking the chocolates for quality. At the end of the aisle you are treated to a taste of handmade chocolate—either milk, white, or dark.

After you get your free piece of non-preservative-filled chocolate, you go into the best room in the house—the place where all the chocolate is sold. Here in a store decorated with vintage items, such as butter churns and old brown liquor bottles, you can get assortments of packaged chocolate or you can make your own collection by choosing from truffles, satin crèmes, almond clusters, pecan caramel patties, and macadamia nut clusters in either milk or dark chocolate. There are also pecan toffee crisps, coconut delights, chewy and creamy caramels, derbies, and specialty items such as peanut-butter-and-jelly-filled chocolates, just to name a few. If you'd prefer to combine two indulgences at once—chocolate and liquor—you can do that as well, because they have chocolates flavored with rum, amaretto, orange liquor, Irish bourbon, or coffee liquor.

Being part of Mars, Ethel M Chocolates is a family-owned company, with a huge emphasis on family. "Some of the people in the kitchen have been here for twenty years," says Lindsay. People stay because Ethel M Chocolates is simply a great place to work. Just ask Steve Bowdin, who after retiring as the factory supervisor, went on to work as the curator for Ethel M Chocolates' Botanical Cactus Garden located just outside the factory doors. "Mars is a good company to work for," he says. Instead of running the factory floor, Steve now works outside taking care of over three hundred species of plants on display in the fifteen thousand cubic yards that make up the free garden. "I've always had a passion for landscaping," says Steve, who actually majored in Agricultural Business. Working in a cactus garden, however, does have its drawbacks. "We get poked and prodded every day of the year," he says. "Practically everything has thorns and needles, but you learn how to deal with it." It's a job Steve loves. "I get to spend all day, every day outside playing in the dirt," he says. "It's like I'm a kid again."

The chocolate factory and the cactus garden is perhaps one of Las Vegas's best-kept secrets. Locals hold it dear, mainly because Ethel M Chocolates stays involved with the community. One event people look forward to all year happens around Christmastime. While many towns decorate their trees and houses with bright, flashing lights, Ethel M Chocolates instead decorates its cacti and then invites the community to enjoy the lights for free, something they have been doing for the past twenty years. "It's a big attraction," says Steve, who's in charge of delicately placing the more than 500,000 lights on the cacti. So whether you come for a taste of chocolates the way they should be made or to see the world's largest collection of drought-tolerant plants, cacti, and succulents, Ethel M Chocolates is the place to go. And if you're worried about your chocolates melting in the dessert heat, don't. They'll happily give you ice packs for free.

FARM BASKET

6148 W. CHARLESTON BLVD. • LAS VEGAS, NV 89146

(702) 878-6343 • FARMBASKETCHICKEN.COM

Carried Away with Quality

Go to any town in America and you'll find a KFC, Church's, or Popeye's, but only in Las Vegas will you find a Farm Basket. What's that you say? You've never heard of Farm Basket Chicken and Turkey? Well, you have no idea what you've been missing. Although the quiet little restaurant has been in Las Vegas since 1977, its roots go back to San Diego, where the first store opened in 1973. At the time, the family-owned and -operated restaurant was known as Picnic and Chicken. By perfecting a secret recipe of herbs and spices, the restaurant was able to make great fried chicken at reasonable prices. In no time the single restaurant grew to twenty-five, and a chain was born.

Right from the start Picnic and Chicken was an innovator in the field of fried chicken and service. In 1973, the company was the first to offer a drive-through window. They were also the first fast-food chicken chain to offer skinless chicken—which they call Skinny Chicken—and a turkey breast sandwich. "Our number-one seller is the Great Gobbler," says Farm Basket owner Steve Perreault, referring to the sandwich that features a breaded turkey breast, Miracle Whip, and cranberry sauce.

In 1977 the chain expanded into Las Vegas, and by 1979 they had opened seven freestanding stores and several others located in food markets. The key to their success was their simplicity. A three-piece dinner gives you just that, three pieces of batter-fried chicken—one leg, one piece of white meat, and one piece of dark meat—mashed potatoes, gravy, coleslaw, and a glazed roll. "We felt a little pressure to keep up with the other places," says Steve, "but in the end we've changed very little." Keeping it simple turned out to be the key to the chain's success. "We found we knew how to do chicken and we do it pretty good," says Steve. "So we stuck with that."

However, moving to a town like Las Vegas did require the chain to make one minor, albeit important, change. Because of the weather conditions in San Diego, all the Picnic and Chicken locations were designed without lobbies. People either went through the drive-through or they walked up to windows, ordered their food, and ate it outside at the tables and chairs the restaurant provided. That model just wasn't going to work in a town where summer temps could get as high as 120 degrees. "We didn't have lobbies in San Diego," says Steve. "We had to add them to the Las Vegas restaurants because it was so hot."

As the years passed, the restaurant remained a fixture in Las Vegas. Family plans changed and eventually Steve and his wife—who was part of the original family of owners—had a chance to not only buy the chain, but the company that made their spices as well. The name was changed to Farm Basket Chicken and Turkey and Steve kept two stores open—the original one on Tropicana and one on Charleston. When the owner of the Tropicana property wanted far

Vintage Spot

McCafe: EST. 1990

Long before Ronald McDonald there was Speedee, the original mascot who had a hamburger for a head. While Speedee
may be long gone in most of America, you can still find him
at this classic McDonalds, which is a replica of the original
drive-up style opened in the 1950s. The building, which has a
'55 Chevy parked out front, uses the Speedee mascot on all
its signage and on a freestanding clock located on a pole in
front of the store.

2248 Paradise Rd.; (702) 796-0664

too much for rent, Steve and his wife closed the place and concentrated entirely on the Charleston location.

The restaurant is a throwback to simpler days when modern
technology wasn't the name of the game. There are no fancy lighted
menus, just a painted board above the ordering window. The decor,
which is early Western farm, has hidden items that celebrate certain
members of the family. For example, a jar of canned beans sits on a
shelf above the door. The jar, and the blue ribbon next to it, is from
Steve's mother-in-law who was a champion canner.

The person who takes your order doesn't enter it into a fancy
computer. Instead, it's marked with a grease pencil on a large board
that rests just above and to the right of the cash register. Farm Basket isn't the kind of place where the owner sits back and collects a
check. Oh no, an apron-clad Steve is behind the counter almost every
day cooking chicken, filling drinks, working the register, and taking
orders. Farm Basket's food, combined with their great service, is what
keeps people coming. "We have an extremely loyal customer base,"
says Steve proudly. "The locals seek us out and come on a regular
basis." They come for the service and they come for the food. What
other fast-food restaurant do you know that makes all its own food
from scratch? "None of our chicken is frozen," says Steve. "We make
our own gravy and salads, all from scratch."

If you ask Steve the secret to his success, he'll tell you to come into work every day, don't go in for fads, and make sure everything is done the old-fashioned way. "We don't go for shtick," he says. "We're not for everybody, but we're good enough for most people." Farm Basket's goal is to provide "great service and great food to every customer." As Steve puts it, "Be fair, be fast, be fresh, and you'll be fine."

Farm Basket is a restaurant that doesn't need to be trendy. They're happy being "the quiet foremost innovator in the fast-food industry." It's a simple business philosophy, one that has worked for more than thirty years. And the proof, as they say, is in the pudding—or in this case, the chicken. Last year Farm Basket showed record sales. In fact, they've had twenty-five consecutive years of record sales. How many fast-food restaurants do you know that can say that?

FRANKIE'S TIKI ROOM

1712 W. CHARLESTON BLVD. • LAS VEGAS, NV 89102

(702) 385-3110 • FRANKIESTIKIROOM.COM

Thank God the Tiki Bar is Open

It's not often you find a place that is both classic and irreverent, or one that is steeped in tradition while being only a few years old. But then again, how many authentic tiki bars can you find in a place like Las Vegas? The answer: one. Located a short distance from the Strip is the only twenty-four-hour, seven-day-a-week tiki bar in the whole of Las Vegas, and like its colorful owner, P. Moss, Frankie's Tiki Room is definitely one of a kind.

You might think "Frankie's" is a strange name for a tiki bar, especially since the owner's name is not now, nor has it ever been, Frankie. But the name, like many aspects of the bar, is part of its charm. Long before Polynesian pop found its way to the city of sin, Frankie's Bar & Cocktail Lounge was a Las Vegas landmark, frequented by casino employees, cab drivers, and locals all looking to let off a bit of steam after a long, hard day. The original Frankie's opened, most likely, in 1955, though records of its original opening—like records of its original owner—have long since been lost to the ages. So too has the source of its original namesake. Some claim Frankie's was named after Frank Sinatra, while others claim it was named after the wife of the original owner. While both are most likely wrong, the second option has the best chance of accuracy.

Throughout the years Frankie's Bar & Cocktail Lounge remained in business—albeit with different owners—from its opening day well into the 1990s, when it began to fall into disrepair. But P. Moss, an ex-bartender and owner of the Double Down Saloon in both Las Vegas and New York, had always kept an eye on the little bar. "It was exactly

what I wanted," he explains. "A stand-alone building with a little character." Moss had plans for a remodel of the bar even before it went up for sale. "I designed it on a napkin while it was still the old Frankie's," Moss says. So when its ninety-some-year-old owner put Frankie's up for sale, Moss jumped at the chance. He bought the little bar and was in escrow within two hours.

Moss and his business partner—and fellow bartender—Chris Andrasfay had always talked about the need for a tiki bar. "Las Vegas didn't have a tiki bar, and every place needs a tiki bar," says Moss. While Las Vegas may seem a strange place for such a bar, the fact is, the escapism associated with the Polynesian culture has long been a mainstay in Las Vegas. It all began way back in 1960 when large men clad in expensive suits paid a visit to Walt Disney and effectively stole his chief designer, California beachcomber Eli Hedley. Hedley made a name for himself creating furniture and functional art from driftwood found on the beach. Walt brought Hedley to Anaheim so that he could work on portions of Adventureland and eventually the Enchanted Tiki Room.

It was while working for Disney that Hedley was approached by representatives of the Stardust Casino, which was run by Morris Barney "Moe" Dalitz, a known mob associate. Hedley was "commissioned" to create the exterior decor of the casino's soon-to-be-opened Polynesian-themed restaurant Aku Aku. Dalitz supplied Hedley with three thirty-foot blocks of featherstone from a quarry in northern Nevada from which he was to carve Moai idols, such as the kind seen on Easter Island. Hedley's amazing carvings became part of the Aku Aku's marketing campaign, showing up on everything from advertisements to matchbook covers. The restaurant was a huge success and a popular nightspot with both tourists and locals until 1980 when the casino underwent a remodel, eliminating the tiki theme entirely.

In 1962 the Sahara Hotel and Casino also cashed in on the tiki culture by opening Don the Beachcomber, a Polynesian-themed restaurant originated by adventurer Donn Beach in 1934. This restaurant, which served exotic cocktails and Polynesian food, also hosted dancing into the wee hours of the morning. While not as popular as the Aku Aku, Don the Beachcomber did enjoy its fair share of popularity until it too was closed in the mid-1980s.

Although one of Hedley's original Moai idols can still be seen resting on a tiny island in the not-so-big pond at Sunset Park, the tiki culture in Las Vegas had all but left by the 1990s. Then along came the Taboo Cove at the Venetian Resort Hotel Casino. Built in 2001, this tiki-themed bar was the first authentic tiki bar built in America since the early 1970s. And while the bar, according to Moss, was "an eye-filling combination of the traditional and the vividly hip," it would only last four years before its doors were shut for good.

With the tiki theme seemingly doomed to remain in Las Vegas's past, attempting to build an authentic tiki bar seemed more like a fool's errand than a sound business idea, but Moss was never one to allow obstacles to dissuade him from an idea. However, almost from the start it seemed as if the stars, both literally and figuratively, were against him. Moss and Andrasfay approached many of the world's elite tiki carvers to create the decor, but time and time again those stars declined. And because authenticity was the goal, the road suddenly looked very difficult indeed. Then came a savior of sorts in the form of a fellow tiki lover.

Bamboo Ben, as he was known, was a frequent patron to one of Moss's other establishments, the Double Down. When Bamboo heard Moss's idea and saw his napkin sketch, he was immediately on board. But Bamboo Ben was no simple tiki lover. He was one of the foremost builders of tiki bars and just happened to be the grandson of Eli Hedley. When Bamboo Ben came on board, all the tiki carvers who had once turned Moss down suddenly made him a priority and the bar quickly came together.

And come together it did. As soon as you pass the Moai idol protecting the front door you are transported into a world much different from the one you left on the other side of the door. From the moment you walk in you find yourself face-to-face with a giant tiki, only this tiki has huge red dice where its eyes should be. Making your way around the bar, you'll find puffer fish lights, a zombie manikin hanging from the ceiling, hundred-year-old tapa cloth for wallpaper, a thatched roof inside the bar, and a little taste of south-sea exotica. You'll also find fixtures made from rattan and bamboo, as well as art from many different tiki artists hanging on the wall. With the bar in perfect shape, the only thing Moss had left to do was name the place. "I was nervous about the name." Moss explains. "I didn't want to be the guy who took something, gutted it, and changed the name. So I just added Tiki Room" and Frankie's Tiki Room was born.

Frankie's Tiki Room is visited by people from all over the world and the bar has quickly become a must-see destination for those visiting Las Vegas. And while the decor is, in a word, tiki-riffic, what Frankie's has really become known for is their amazing drink menu, one that mixes the classics with sixty of Frankie's own mad creations such as the Thurston Howl, the Fink Bomb, and Three Rum Scum. These drinks can be served in a regular glass or in Frankie's signature tiki mugs. "Vegas kitsch," as Moss likes to put it. There are multiple mugs to choose from and depending on the drink ordered, you can get a tiki bandit mug shaped more like a slot machine than an idol; a four-armed woman; a fat-bellied tiki sitting on a large die; or a tiki with vicious teeth and skeleton arms that looks more like it's ready to make a meal out of you than for you to drink out of it.

Incidentally, Moss never received any backlash about the name from any of the original Frankie's longtime patrons. "Keeping the name meant everything," Moss says. "I'm really happy I kept the name." Frankie's has lived on. And while it may have been given a facelift, the bar is still standing and, most would agree, is better than ever. So if you're looking for the traditional combined with the irreverent, take a trip to the Tiki Room and tell them Frankie sent you.

FREED'S BAKERY

9815 S. EASTERN • LAS VEGAS, NV 89183

(702) 456-7762 • FREEDSBAKERY.COM

The Sweet Side of Sin . . . City

At one time in America when you wanted meat you went to a butcher, when you wanted produce you went to a market, and when you wanted sweets you went to a bakery. These places were quaint, small, and typically serviced only one neighborhood; and because they were most often operated by people who also lived in that same neighborhood, when you came in, much like *Cheers*, everyone knew your name. These places thrived, not by simply knowing their customers' names, but by also knowing their likes, habits, and favorites. In short, they understood the customer was their lifeline and they treated each person who entered their shops accordingly.

But then came grocery stores, supermarkets, and big-box chains. And while these stores may have brought lower prices and convenience, they also brought frozen foods, large quantities, and impersonal service. As these stores took over the neighborhoods once serviced by butchers, bakers, and candlestick makers, one by one the local neighborhood stores disappeared. That is, except for one—Freed's Bakery. Strangely enough, the bakery was started not by a baker, but by a musician.

Milton Fried—pronounced with a long "e"—was born in Hoboken, New Jersey. In the late 1930s he was a saxophonist playing at the Rustic Cabin, a venue in Englewood Cliffs where such notables as the Andrews Sisters and a then-unknown Ol' Blue Eyes played regularly. When the Japanese bombed Pearl Harbor in 1941, Fried put down his saxophone and picked up a gun, fighting for freedom in the US Army. After he was discharged, he returned to his home and headed to the

big city of New York looking for work. He found it and for the next thirteen years he played Broadway in such notable shows as *Finian's Rainbow*, *Gentlemen Prefer Blondes*, and *Pal Joey*.

However, Fried also had a secret life. During the night Fried was a saxophonist on Broadway, but during the day he was a restaurateur. Outside of Englewood Cliffs, New Jersey, on Route 9W sat a large barn-shaped building with MILT FREED'S RED BARN painted in large letters on the side. There Milt and his wife Esther served hamburgers, hot pastrami, country chicken, and Alderny ice cream. They changed the spelling of their last name to a phonetic pronunciation in order to avoid people thinking everything in the restaurant was "fried." The restaurant was so popular it routinely caused traffic jams on the Bergen County country roads.

By 1959 Milt and Esther had five children and were looking for a change of venue. They decided a relocation to Los Angeles was in order, so they packed up all their worldly belongings, piled their children into the backseat of the car, and headed down the road. But they never made it. On their way to Los Angeles Milt and Esther stopped in Las Vegas—a town whose population almost doubled every weekend. The couple saw the potential the booming town of Las Vegas had to offer and immediately unpacked the car.

Vintage Spot

CARLO'S BAKERY: EST. 2014

While Buddy Valastro may have just opened his bakery in Las Vegas, his original New Jersey bakery has been in business since 1910. Valastro brings his tried and true recipes to Las Vegas, saving you a trip to Jersey.

Grand Canal Shoppes, 3325 Las Vegas Blvd. South; (702) 607-2356; bakeshop.carlosbakery.com

Once in Vegas, Milt began anew his double life. He hooked up with his old Rustic Cabin buddy who was now running with a different kind of "pack" at the Sands Hotel & Casino on the Las Vegas Strip. Fried played saxophone, bassoon, and oboe in the Copa Room while Frank, Dean, and Sammy performed nightly. During the day, however, Milt and his wife managed an eleven-seat snack bar called Freed's Royal Pastries at the Panorama Market, which was owned by city commissioner Harry Leny. The problem was that neither Milt nor Esther was a baker. To solve this dilemma Esther bought doughnuts every morning from the Spudnut Doughnut Shop down the street, brought them back to the snack bar, and sold them for a profit.

They were so successful that six weeks later Leny bought the couple a six-pan oven, a thirty-quart mixer, and a refrigerator—and Freed's Bakery was born. Almost from the start Milt and Esther specialized in cakes. Even in the late 1950s Vegas was already becoming a wedding destination and the Frieds understood the opportunity making cakes presented. Bakers from around the country passed though Las Vegas on a regular basis and Milt gave all who asked an opportunity to bake for him. "Show me what you can do," he told each baker, instructing them to make their favorite item. Those that made the cut were hired.

While Milt may not have been a baker, he did know how to treat the people who came into his bakery. "Don't worry about pleasing the customers," he told his bakers. "Please me and let me worry about pleasing the customers." And please them he did. Between 1960 and

1962 Milt and his wife opened seven more Freed's Royal Pastry shops in Las Vegas. While the Frieds were becoming known for their pastries, cookies, and cakes, their French bread was by far their biggest seller. At their shop on the Strip near the Sahara Hotel & Casino lines would form every morning in anticipation of the 7 a.m. opening. Customers—which consisted mainly of casino employees, business executives, and even showgirls—would buy out the bread within fifteen minutes of opening.

In 1970 Milt and Esther decided to step away from the hands-on running of the business, eventually leaving it in the very capable hands of their youngest daughter Joni and their grandson Max Jacobson-Fried. Over the years the bakery has remained, keeping many of its original recipes, while Las Vegas itself has grown from a small town to a major city. For more than thirty years it has been named Best Bakery in the *Las Vegas Review-Journal*'s Best of Las Vegas and has also been named Best of Weddings—Wedding Cakes & Desserts by *The Knot*. Additionally, Freed's has played host to many Food Network stars and television shows, having appeared on Rachael Ray's *Tasty Travels* and *$40 a Day* and Warren Brown's *Sugar Rush*, as well as *Food Finds* and *Fabulous Cakes* seasons 1 and 2.

In 2011, having been hit by a bad economy, Freed's consolidated all its stores into one brand new, larger location. Yet people still come from all over the valley to get their just desserts. The bakery, which no longer serves bread, has chosen to focus mainly on cakes, cookies, and pastries. However, everything is still made from scratch. "We stick to the basics," explains grandson Max. "We do what we do best and don't get too fancy." It is a sentiment echoed by patrons to the bakery. "It's just too sinful for words," says one of Freed's customers between bites of strawberry shortcake (the bakery's best seller). "I won't eat like this every day, but I'm eating like this today."

What hasn't changed, what is most likely the secret to the bakery's fifty-four years of success, is the way Freed's treats their customers. "I watched my grandmother and aunts handle and treat customers," Max explains. "It's still the way we treat customers to this day." It is clear that the people who come into the bakery are just as important today as they were to Milt and Esther all those years ago. So much so that it is Max's own personal cell phone number on the after-hours message.

GAMBLERS GENERAL STORE

800 S. MAIN ST. • LAS VEGAS, NV 89101
(702) 382-9903 • GAMBLERSGENERALSTORE.COM

Dice Dice, Baby

*J*f you want to win at the tables in any Las Vegas casino you can go to your bank, withdraw your nest egg, rush to the casino, turn the nest egg into gaming chips, play at the tables, and hope you brought enough to get you over the severe learning curve before you go broke—not likely. Or you could simply go to the Gamblers General Store in downtown Las Vegas and purchase one of the more than three thousand books they have on the subject. Better yet, you could buy everything you need to start your own card game (table, chairs, felt, card shoe, deck of cards), take it all back to your home, and invite your friends, and their nest eggs, to come over to play a little no-limit Texas Hold 'em.

While the last option may get you into more trouble than its worth, it is possible to find these items and more among the over fifteen thousand gambling products available for purchase at one of the most unique stores in all of Las Vegas. Want to buy a poker table? You can. Want to buy a twenty-one table? You can. Heck, you can even buy a craps table if you have the room. Want to customize your own felt—the green part of the gaming table? They got you covered. Want to start a bingo parlor? You can do that. Need some customized poker chips? No problem. Dice? They got it. In fact, if it involves gambling or games of chance, Gamblers General Store has everything you could possibly need.

Opened in 1984, the Gamblers General Store has become the one-stop shop for gamblers and wannabe gamblers from all over the world. And while the store carries everything your little gambling heart could desire, they specialize in cards, dice, books, and poker chips. When Hollywood needs chips for television series like *The Sopranos* and *CSI* or movies such as *Casino, Ocean's 11,* and *Rush Hour 2,* they turn to Gamblers General Store. "We specialize in custom chips," says Avery Cardoza, the current owner. "We used to make the actual chip, but now we just put customized labels on them." Cardoza, who bought the place in December of 2013, has big plans for the growing store. He brought in specialized equipment that can print the label and then attach those printed labels to the chips—allowing people or companies to put any logo they want on a gaming chip. His stock allows you to choose from traditional casino chip colors—beige or blue = $1, red = $5, green = $25, and black = $100—or a rainbow of other colors that match your logo, your store, or whatever you want them to match.

You want playing cards? You just have to tell them what kind. Every deck imaginable from every major company that makes cards is on display. They have zombie, Marvel, pharaoh, Alice of Wonderland, haunted, steampunk, skull, and 184 other types of decks from Bicycle, Bee, Copag, Ellusionist, Karnival, and Kem, to name but a few. And these aren't the cards you'd find in the aisle of a grocery store or on the discount rack of a chain store. No siree, these cards are the good decks. The ones that feel like silk in your hands, the ones that are coated to make them glide off the tips of a dealer's fingers as she slides the card across the twenty-one table over to your spot. These cards are quality decks.

But let's say you're itchin' to host a casino night and you want to use actual cards from the Golden Nugget, the 4 Queens, the El Cortez, or Binion's. Gamblers General Store is your place. What you may not know is that casinos go through hundreds of decks of cards every day. To prevent cards from being marked, and to get rid of cards that may have been worn, torn, or otherwise damaged, the casino rotates old cards with new cards on a very regular basis. The old cards—the ones that were actually played on the table games—are then sold in the casino gift shops or at Gamblers General Store.

If you're wondering how a casino could possibly sell a deck of cards with their logo on it and prevent someone from marking the cards and then reintroducing them into play, it's simple. The casino beats you to the punch by marking the cards themselves. In the past

this was done by drilling a small, button-sized hole into the center of the deck, an obvious indication that the deck has been used. However, when people complained that the drilling was going through the casino's logo, the casino switched tactics and began cutting corners—literally—off the decks. These cards too would be easy to spot if anyone were foolish enough to try to reintroduce them into play.

But maybe cards aren't your thing. Maybe you're into dice. Well, you've come to the right place. Gamblers General Store has specialty dice, novelty dice, and precision dice—or the kind used in all casinos. Precision dice have been carefully cut so their shape and balance are more accurate than regular dice. The dots—called pips—on precision dice are flat, not dimpled, and like the playing cards, the casinos change their dice frequently. The dice are so important to the casino, they are kept in a locked vault that can only be entered by two people at the same time—typically a pit boss and a security officer. Every single die is accounted for and when they are taken out of play, like cards, they are marked and sold. You can find the dice of many different casinos at the store, even rare dice from casinos no longer in business.

And if you're thinking of taking those dice back to the craps table, you might first want to look at the pips representing the number four, as it is there where you will most likely find the barely visible mark the casino placed on the dice to indicate they are used and not eligible for replay. And if you're thinking of taking your chances with these "marked" cards or dice, just remember that cheating is something the casinos and the police do not take lightly. But if you do decide to "roll the dice," they'll be happy to show you a sight not every tourist gets to see . . . the inside of a jail cell.

THE GOLDEN GATE HOTEL & CASINO

1 FREMONT ST. • LAS VEGAS, NV 89101

(702) 385-1906 • GOLDENGATECASINO.COM

Where It All Began

In Las Vegas, history can be hard to come by. Want to enjoy a show and a drink in the original Copa Room made famous by the Rat Pack and the Copa Girls? You can't—it's no longer there. Want to see the Dunes with its thirty-five-foot fiberglass sultan? You can't—we blew it up. Want to see the New Frontier, the Desert Inn, the Castaways, the Thunderbird, the Hacienda, the Aladdin, Bourbon Street, the Boardwalk, or the Stardust? Tough luck; we imploded those places long, long ago. However, if you're undaunted in your desire to find a bit of original Las Vegas, there is one place you can go: the Golden Gate Casino.

If the address doesn't clue you in, a trip to downtown Las Vegas will certainly do the trick. Entering the Golden Gate you find a casino decorated with rich, dark wood, much like the casinos of old. Photos of the Rat Pack adorn the walls adjacent to the gaming tables, which are manned by dealers dressed in 1920s-era outfits, complete with garter armbands. A saloon-style wooden bar rests against the wall on the other side of the table games—an area known as "the pit." The ceiling above the pit is constructed of copper-colored, decorative metal tiles, which add a flair of both richness and vintage to the gaming area. In fact, except for the modern slot machines, it's easy to get the feel of how the casino must have looked back in 1906.

The property on which the Golden Gate Casino stands was originally purchased in a land auction on May 15, 1905, for $1,750. The auction was held by brothers William Clark and J. Ross Clark, the latter of which was a banker and successful miner. It was J. Ross's idea to form a railroad and run it from Salt Lake City to California. The railroad would not only be able to move quartz and copper from Montana, it could also move the newly discovered gold and silver in Nevada, and anything else that needed to be transported to and from the southwest. In order to do that, however, the brothers needed a place to stop and water the steam boilers of the train's engine. William scouted out the area and found a large ranch owned by Helen J. Stewart. William talked Stewart into selling a large portion of her land. The brothers held a two-day auction to sell the land and Las Vegas was born.

Less than a year later, the Hotel Nevada—which would eventually become the Golden Gate Casino—opened on the land purchased in the auction. The hotel was one of the first to open as an actual brick building in Las Vegas—a building that still stands to this day. A local newspaper described the hotel at its opening as being "as comfortable a hostelry as can be found anywhere." Rooms at the hotel could be purchased for one dollar a night. They were large by 1906 standards—ten feet by ten feet—and featured electric lighting, ventilation, and steam-heat radiators. The hotel also featured the first telephone

in Las Vegas. To reach the hotel all you had to do was ask the operator to "Ring 1, please." Of course, at the time you also had to wait for other phones to be installed and the operators to be hired.

In 1909 Nevada took the strange step of outlawing gambling, causing all the hotels in Las Vegas to get out the mothballs and put away their gambling devices. The decision would be wisely overturned in 1931 when the state began issuing gambling licenses. During that time, Fremont Street—the road in front of the hotel—was paved for the first time. The hotel also installed an outdoor electric sign, which would become the precursor of sign advertising in Las Vegas. In 1931 the hotel made the rather bewildering—and still unexplained—move of changing its name to Sal Sagev, which was simply "Las Vegas" spelled backward.

In 1955 the hotel was sold to a group of Italian-Americans—Italo Ghelfi, Robert Picardo, Al Durante, Leo Massaro, and Dan Fiorito—from San Francisco. The hotel's name was once again changed, this time to its current Golden Gate Casino. Two years later the Golden Gate Casino began selling shrimp cocktails, featuring oversized shrimp stuffed into a six-ounce, tulip-shaped glass filled with cocktail sauce and a wedge of lemon. The dish, which sold for fifty cents, became a Las Vegas tradition for close to thirty years. In fact, thirty-two years later when the hotel sold its twenty-five millionth shrimp cocktail, it was celebrated with an event that brought together the four mayors who had served during the years the dish was sold.

In 1964 the casino got a facelift. However, instead of imploding the building as is the current trend, the original rooms located in the original hotel were kept and updated. The outside of the hotel also received a modern look, with the historical exterior being left in place under the façade.

In 1990 Italo Ghelfi's sons bought out all partners and took over the property. One of their first acts was to restore the building, removing the façade erected in 1964 and restoring the exterior to its original look. The hotel has taken great strides to hold on to its past while still pioneering the future. The past is artfully captured in wood display cases in the lobby. These cases hold a telephone directory, a set of hand towels, and a room key—an actual metal key—to the hotel when it bore the name Sal Sagev. There you can also find a replica of the original telephone and a piece of wood, unearthed from Fremont

Street in front of the hotel, that held the original telephone line. There is also a gaming ledger for a twenty-one game and a hotel ledger both from the original Hotel Nevada and both from 1907.

Just off the lobby is a set of seven slot machines from the early days of the Golden Gate Casino. One of the machines, a quarter machine, paid out one hundred coins for a jackpot; twenty were paid by the machine and the balance by the attendant. A machine to the left of the quarter machine had a grand prize of one hundred dollars, which could be won with a dollar bet. A sign on the machine promoted what is now a Las Vegas staple: FREE COCKTAILS WHILE PLAYING ASK WAITRESS.

On October 11, 2010, the largest bet on a roulette table in Las Vegas history was placed at the Golden Gate. The bet was made by the cast members of MTV's *The Buried Life*, a show that follows four young men as they complete a bucket list of one hundred things to do before they die. Number 75 on their list was to try to win one million dollars. The attempt at wining the million dollars started with a $125,000 bet on a roulette table. The bet was placed on red at even money. The dealer spun the ball at the top of the roulette wheel and when the ball stopped, it had landed on red.

The young men had just won $225,000, which they immediately bet again, only this time on black. This second bet became the largest ever placed on a roulette table—beating the previous bet by $5,000. As the dealer spun the small white ball a second time, one of the young men stood on a chair and asked everyone in the casino to root for them in their attempt at the million. As bystanders cheered and four young men held their breath, the ball slowly spun around the top of the roulette table before bouncing down into the combination of colors and numbers, finally coming to a stop . . . on red.

GOLDEN STEER STEAKHOUSE

308 W. SAHARA AVE. • LAS VEGAS, NV 89102

(702) 384-4470 • GOLDENSTEERSTEAKHOUSELASVEGAS.COM

The Best Steaks on Earth

*J*n 1958 when the Golden Steer Steakhouse opened its doors, there wasn't much around. The El Rancho was across the street and sitting kitty-corner was the Sahara Hotel and Casino. In a couple of years down the road, the Honest John Casino would open on the corner of Sahara and the Strip before being replaced by the Big Wheel Casino, then the Centerfold Casino, and finally the Jolly Trolley Restaurant, Saloon and Dining Depot. Other than the few stores in the shopping plaza itself, there was little else but desert. Every one of those places has come and gone, but the Golden Steer Steakhouse is still around.

When Vegas was in its infancy, gourmet dining wasn't a focus. It's not that fine dining wasn't available—each casino typically had a cafe and a restaurant where coat-and-tie-clad gentlemen and gown-adorned women ate while staying at the property. The food was good, but it wasn't the casino's emphasis. At the time, gambling, drinking, and entertainment were the prime focus. As casinos evolved into mega-resorts, food became a priority. Modern Las Vegas casinos have restaurants owned and operated by Wolfgang Puck, Emeril Lagasse, Bobby Flay, Hubert Keller, and Tom Colicchio.

So how does a restaurant stay in business for more than half a century in a world where famous chefs are the name of the game? It's a combination of quality and history. "We create an environment that's one of a kind," says Dr. Michael J. Signorelli, who bought the Golden Steer in 2001. "We're like a restaurant inside a museum." But it's not a stuffy museum, one where you're afraid to touch anything.

It's a museum that invites you in, asks you how you're doing, and serves you a drink, after seating you in a booth whose benches were once graced by bottoms belonging to the likes of Frank Sinatra, Sammy Davis Jr., Dean Martin, and Marilyn Monroe. *Bon Appétit* magazine described the Golden Steer as "a taste of vanishing Vegas" when it listed the restaurant as one of its Top Ten Must-Visit Classic Restaurants in 2009.

The Golden Steer Steakhouse is a throwback to a time when restaurants were famous for their service and the quality of their food, not who owned them. This, in fact, is how the Golden Steer became a Las Vegas icon. Vegas in the 1960s was a segregated community. Entertainers like Sammy Davis Jr. could perform in the showroom, but couldn't stay in the hotel, walk around the casino, or eat in the casino's restaurants. Sammy had to stay in a boardinghouse in west Las Vegas. One night, on his way to the Moulin Rouge—a casino built specifically for African Americans—he spied the large, gold-colored steer on the sign outside the restaurant and decided to stop in. At the time you could enjoy a plate of homemade sausage for $3.25, a lobster tail for $4.00, or a large slice of prime rib for $4.95.

The next time Sammy came in he brought Frank, Deano, and Joey Bishop. The group would bring with them friends and sometimes family, taking up four entire booths. Every time the Rat Pack came in they sat at the same four booths. Those booths—which still boast their original leather—are now marked with a plaque carrying the names and photos of their famous occupants.

After the Rat Pack made the Golden Steer their home, word got out and all manner of famous people made their way to the restaurant. "Everybody started coming in here and everyone wanted their own booth," says Dr. Signorelli. John Wayne, Joe DiMaggio, Marilyn Monroe, and Elvis Presley have all been regular customers at the Golden Steer and all have booths in their honor. Long after their divorce, Monroe and DiMaggio used to come in together, but sat at booths directly across from each other. At one point, for a reason lost to history, DiMaggio changed his booth to what was then the front of the restaurant, leaving Marilyn in the back. Ironically, the entrance of the restaurant was changed and Marilyn's booth is now in the front, while Joe's is in the back. This trend of the famous coming to the steak house didn't end after the Rat Pack left town. Clint Eastwood has a booth and Las Vegas resident Nicolas Cage is a regular, as is Mario Andretti, Mayor Carolyn Goodman, and her ex-mayoral husband Oscar.

The Golden Steer was also the go-to place during Vegas's mob era. At that time the restaurant had a back door that led to a private room that could be shut off from the rest of the diners. This room—now known as "the mob room"—was frequented by the likes of Tony "the Ant" Spilotro and Morris Barney "Moe" Dalitz. At times the restaurant, which was then owned by Joe Calujan, didn't even know who was in the back room, the door being closed even to the staff.

As time went by, the restaurant fell on hard times and Calujan eventually declared bankruptcy. That was when Dr. Signorelli stepped in. "I bought this place because of the history," he says. "It lost some of its luster and food quality, so I started buying the best steaks money could buy." In fact, prime steaks are the only grade of steak served at the Golden Steer. Meat is purchased by the half cow and cut on the premises, which is why the Golden Steer bills its steaks as "the best on Earth."

Once the ink dried on the ownership papers, Dr. Signorelli began sprucing up the place. Instead of remodeling, he kept the ambience and charm that made the Golden Steer a hit originally. The decor can

✮Vintage Spot

BOB TAYLOR'S ORIGINAL RANCH HOUSE and SUPPER CLUB: EST. 1955

Just as the name says, this restaurant is in an actual ranch house. It's even located in the heart of a residential community, making it not particularly easy to find. Going to the Ranch House is like taking a step back into the old West—complete with saddles. Which, actually, is what Vegas was like when the restaurant got its start in 1955—making it the oldest restaurant in the Vegas valley.

6250 Rio Vista St.; (702) 645-1399; bobtaylorsranchhouse.com

best be described as Old West meets casino lounge. Wood-paneled walls are decorated with paintings by C. M. Russell and famous western artifacts. Behind the hostess stand rests an authentic 1866 Navy Arms Yellow Boy rifle. Just above Clint Eastwood's booth sit two six-guns and the holster once owned by Las Vegas's most famous sheriff: Ralph Lamb. A set of steer horns is mounted above the entryway to the dining area and another set is mounted at the back of the room. There are both black leather booths and red leather booths, depending on which dining room you are in.

History abounds at the Golden Steer Steakhouse. Where else in Las Vegas can you be cooked a meal by the very same person who once cooked for Frank, Sammy, and Dean? "Our chefs have been here for twenty-five years," says manager Stephanie Steel. Stephanie, who now makes her home at the Golden Steer, owned a successful restaurant in town for seventeen years. If you ask Stephanie to tell you the best part of her job, she'll say it's the guests. "I sit down with people all the time who tell me their stories," she says. The Golden Steer can also claim something no other restaurant on the Strip can—they can flambé Cherries Jubilee or Bananas Fosters right at the table, just as in the old days. While a city ordinance currently prohibits such flames at the dining table, the Golden Steer was grandfathered in because it has been doing these table-side desserts ever since it opened in 1958.

Going strong for close to fifty-six years, the Golden Steer has no plans of slowing down. April 7, 2012, was declared Golden Steer Steakhouse day by the city of Las Vegas and *Forbes* listed the Golden Steer as one of the 12 Great Las Vegas Restaurants. In 2013 the readers of the *Las Vegas Review Journal* voted the restaurant Best Steak House. "People come here from all over the world," says Dr. Signorelli. "We're still adding history to the city."

GUARDIAN ANGEL CATHEDRAL

302 CATHEDRAL WAY • LAS VEGAS, NV 89109

(702) 735-5241 • GACLV.ORG

A Refuge in a City of Sin

Close to forty million people visit Las Vegas every year and you'd expect few, if any, to have plans for attending church during their stay. You would expect that, but you just might be surprised. Casinos offer everything their guests' hearts desire—free drinks, shows, fabulous restaurants, outrageous nightlife—everything, that is, except a place of worship, and that is by design. No one wants their guests contemplating the wages of sin while shuffling dollars into a slot machine, doubling their bid on the craps table, or downing that third (or fourth) three-foot-high margarita. Yet amidst the glitz and glamour on the Las Vegas Strip sits a not-so-tiny refuge from all Sin City has to offer. It's a refuge visited by thousands of people every year.

Of course, like the city in which it resides, this refuge also has a rather nefarious past. The Guardian Angel Cathedral got its start from none other than Morris Barney "Moe" Dalitz—an admitted bootlegger with ties to organized crime. Moe Dalitz came into this world on Christmas Eve, 1899, in Boston, Massachusetts. By the time he was twenty he was using the delivery truck from his father's dry-cleaning business to run bootleg alcohol in Michigan, where the family had moved in 1907. Thirty years later, in 1949, Dalitz was sent to Las Vegas to take over the construction of the Desert Inn Hotel and Casino (now the Wynn) when the original owner, Wilber Smith, ran short of funds. Dalitz would eventually run the Desert Inn upon its completion, as well as both the Showboat and Stardust Casinos.

A year later Dalitz was the target of the famous Kefauver Hearings, which were held in the federal courthouse on Stewart Avenue in downtown Las Vegas. When questioned by Senator Estes Kefauver about his running bootleg alcohol, Dalitz responded, "If you people wouldn't have drunk it, I wouldn't have bootlegged it." But Dalitz was more than a man with ties to organized crime. He was also well known for his philanthropy. During his tenure in Las Vegas, he gave money for the construction of a hospital, a mall, a country club and golf course, a residential track of homes, and even some of the buildings that make up the University of Nevada, Las Vegas. In 1961 Dalitz donated a plot of land just to the north of the Desert Inn. The land was to be used to erect a cathedral. But Dalitz didn't just donate the land, he also funded the entire project.

The design of the building fell to the very capable hands of architect Paul Revere Williams, although Williams was actually an unlikely candidate. An African American born on February 18, 1894 in Los Angeles, Williams was an orphan by the time he was four. Forced into a foster home, he was lucky enough to land with a family who believed in the power of education. Williams, who was the only African American attending Polytechnic High School at the time, was actually discouraged from going into architecture by one of his teachers who was concerned about his ability to attract clients in a

Vintage Spot
ST. anne CHURCH: est. 1966

While not as famous as its larger cousin on the Strip, this little church also bears three mosaics designed by Edith Piczek on the outside of the building. On February 12, 1987, services for Liberace were held at the church. The service was attended by such notable celebrities as Rich Little, Debbie Reynolds, Robert Goulet, and Donald O'Connor.

**1901 S. Maryland Pkwy.; (702) 735-0510;
lasvegas-diocese.org**

mainly white community. This didn't stop Williams from pursuing his dreams. It also didn't stop him from making a name for himself in the 1920s and '30s designing expensive homes for wealthy clients in Bel Air, Brentwood, and Beverly Hills.

Williams chose a dramatic A-frame design for his eleven-hundred-seat cathedral, which has the effect of making the entire building appear as if it's reaching up to the heavens. Above the front door rests an enormous two-thousand-square-foot mosaic designed by Hungarian artist Edith Piczek in 1966. The mosaic, which was executed by mosaic artist L. Favret-Pietrasanta, shows a guardian angel—the cathedral's namesake—with three figures representing Prayer, Penance, and Peace. Piczek also designed the mural that rests behind the altar. This mural, "The Final Beginning," shows "swooping angels" rising up toward heaven around the guardian angel. These angels are depicted in a style—called Mystic Realism by Piczek—that is more consistent with what you'd expect to find drawn on the pages of a comic book than on the wall of a Catholic church. Far from a traditional design, these angels are multicolored in bright yellows, reds, and oranges, highlighted with greens, blues, and purples.

The twelve beautifully colored, triangular stained-glass windows inside the cathedral represent the Stations of the Cross. Created by Edith's sister Isabel Piczek, a Hungarian-trained theoretical physicist and monumental artist, they were designed in the same

Mystic Realism style that is more cubist than traditional. Each window depicts themes that subtly demonstrate the evils of gambling and one even has the 1970s Las Vegas skyline incorporated into it. Each window received donations from different sources, with window XII receiving its funding from actor Danny Thomas and his wife.

For many years, the church attracted tourists and casino employees alike, each looking for an escape from the neon lights of the strip. However, as Las Vegas grew, fewer and fewer employees attended services, leaving only tourists to keep the door open. Through it all, the cathedral has remained a refuge in the city of sin since it was built in 1963 and has even expanded. In 1995 the cathedral underwent a $1.3 million renovation, part of which saw the destruction of the nearby tiki-themed Bali Hai motel.

The cathedral has weekend and weekday masses. It has reconciliations and novenas and on the first Friday of every month in answer to the many Happy Hours held in bars and casinos along the Strip, the cathedral holds a "Holy Hour" following the 12:10 mass. And while Las Vegas has become an example of what unbridled extravagance can lead to, the Guardian Angel Cathedral—as with churches of old—still rings its bell every hour on the hour not only to indicate the time, but also possibly to remind tourists and residents alike that it still dares to stand as a lone beacon in defiance of a city built largely on sin.

An Old-Fashioned Family Business

When he opened his military surplus store in 1973, Larry Hahn had no thoughts of going into that line of work. His mother, Hilda West, was already operating the very successful Hilda's Restaurant and Living Room Lounge and he was working as maître d' at the Sands Hotel and Casino's famous Pavilion Club. It was while working there that Larry struck up a friendship with several military surplus dealers who came to Las Vegas for yearly conventions. The men, appealing to Larry's love of history and historic items, convinced him to take a chance and open a much-needed military surplus store north of the valley in Las Vegas. "They offered to help him get started," says Christina Hahn, Larry's wife. "When we opened the original store up the street, it was only one thousand square feet," she says. Three years later Larry and Christina moved the business down the road a piece to its current location, a building with over fifteen thousand square feet.

A military surplus store may seem an oddity in the city of sin; however, one of the many things people don't know about Las Vegas is that the town played a significant role in helping the world defeat Adolf Hitler. In 1940 the United States government was searching for a place to train the machine gunners who would be assigned to their new B-17 bomber, called the "Flying Fortress," and the B-24 bomber, called the "Liberator." Las Vegas was the perfect choice. The valley was sparsely populated, with only around eight thousand people, and the weather was perfect for year-round training. This meant planes flying over the large desert area posed little danger to the small

community during training activities. This enticed the government to open the Las Vegas Air Gunnery School just north of town. The gunnery school eventually turned into Nellis Air Force Base, and more than seventy years later the military still has a significant impact on Las Vegas's culture.

In no place is this more apparent than Hahn's World of Surplus. Whatever your military needs, Hahn's is your place. If you want a waterproof camouflage raincoat, this is where you'll find it. Need winter camouflage and snowshoes? They're here. Want a green military-issue sleeping bag? They've got those too. If you need wool blankets, netting, or tarps, Hahn's has got you covered. In fact, just about every military clothing need is met at Hahn's. If you want to dress like a Ranger, they've got your clothes. If you're looking for an advanced tactical concealment system, they've got that too. Or if, being in Las Vegas, you prefer desert attire, Hahn's is the place.

Running a military surplus store isn't as much of a stretch as you might think for a former maître d', because Larry was once in the military himself, though he never saw any action. "He was just about ready to go active when he caught rheumatic fever," says Christina. The Navy never accepted him, but instead, gave him a full honorable discharge. It seems, though, that the military was his destiny all along.

While Larry may never have served, he has a keen grasp on the important role the military plays in modern society. He also understands the role it has played throughout history. This is evident all throughout the store, as intermixed with the modern tactical jackets, patches, and pins are remembrances of another time. One of these remembrances comes in the form of a framed 1940 San Francisco newspaper with the headline "Nazi Army in Paris." Underneath the framed paper is a 1919 photo of World War I troops just home from battle. The display case on which these items rest is appropriately dedicated to both World War I and World War II. The case houses such items as a bust of Hitler and a large leather wallet meant to hold discharge papers from World War I. The display also contains a camera lens for a spy plane, bayonets, medals, binoculars, canteens, compasses, goggles, and a red SS arm band. "Many of the items came from concentration camps," Larry explains, adding that he has donated several items to the Holocaust Museum.

Larry doesn't just run a military surplus store; he is also a collector of military history. This is evident in the store's decor. Positioned directly behind and above the checkout counter is an impressive display of military headwear all resting on the heads of proud mannequins. The hats, which date as far back as the Civil War, are both American and foreign. In fact, just about every major country is represented. There are hats from Russia, Germany, Scotland, Australia, and England. The collection, which includes both officer and enlisted headwear, also contains women's hats and Coast Guard hats, as well as old flight caps complete with goggles. There is even a hat from Switzerland, its gray feather still sticking proudly outward from the side.

Beneath the headwear are all manner of swords, each and every one authentic, and representing all time periods—the oldest of which dates back to 1833. Larry also has a collection of firearms, though few of them work. "I don't look for ones that shoot," he says. "I don't want to entice thieves." The rifles and pistols Larry has on display may not shoot, but it doesn't make them any less impressive. Most are in great shape, their wood stocks still intact. Protecting these items is a collection of vintage G.I. Joes, standing at the ready just below the guns, but still high enough to be out of the reach of curious hands.

When walking around Hahn's World of Surplus it's easy to get distracted by camouflage shirts, shorts, and tank tops, military flags, and the large collection of military uniforms, both dress and battle ready. But in doing so, you may miss the history hidden throughout the store. For example, near the back where the military uniforms sit on hangers are a Russian G suit and a 1970s Vietnam-era uniform—both of which are not for sale. In another part of the store you can find a 1945 field pack and cargo bag—they too are not for sale.

However, if you want to go military, there are plenty of items that are for sale. And if you really want that true military experience, you can purchase some K rations. Of course, these K rations have been updated to the needs of a modern society. Instead of the typical meals you might have found in, say, World War II, you can purchase a pork chop with noodles in Jamaican-style sauce in a box. You can also purchase—in a box—an egg omelet with vegetables and cheese or pasta and vegetables in Alfredo-style sauce. These are not your granddaddy's K rations.

While the military is its primary focus, Hahn's isn't just for the military enthusiast. The survivalist, camper, and prospector will also feel perfectly at home amidst the saws, shovels, pickaxes, and machetes. Here you can purchase outdoor cooking supplies such as pots, pans, cups, plates, and, of course, coffee pots. You can also purchase silverware, which you can use to eat your K rations off the same style plates as did Hawkeye Pierce and Trapper John on just about every episode of *M*A*S*H.* Of course, in true Las Vegas style, Hahn's even sells poker chips so you have something to do on those long, cold nights of guard duty.

If you ask Christina how Hahn's has managed to stay in business so long, she'll tell you quite frankly, "We treat everyone like family." In fact, Christina describes the place as "an old-fashioned family business," and it's easy to see why. Everyone at Hahn's is not only knowledgeable, they're about as friendly as they can possibly be. "We've had people coming here for forty years," Christina says. "You can't help but be friends with them."

HISTORIC FREMONT STREET

FREMONT STREET • LAS VEGAS, NV 89101

(702) 678-5600 • VEGASEXPERIENCE.COM

The Second Most Famous
Street in Las Vegas

ost people who come to Las Vegas make plans to stay at one of the casinos on the famous Las Vegas Strip. Unfortunately most of those people leave our fair city without ever having visited its true roots—the place where it all began. While the Strip may be the most famous street in Las Vegas, that's not where Las Vegas first established roots. The first major casino appeared on the Strip in 1942; however, Fremont Street predates that by almost forty years.

As far back as 1881, the Union Pacific planned on laying tracks to connect Salt Lake City to the fast-growing Los Angeles. The rail was slated to follow the Old Spanish Trail, which ran right through Las Vegas. The owners of the Union Pacific Railroad, seeing great opportunity for advancement and profit, installed the rails along the trail. Unfortunately the railroad was not operated well in the 1880s and it fared no better when the financial panic of 1893 hit the United States. By the time the Spanish-American War erupted in 1898 the Union Pacific was on the verge of bankruptcy. It eventually reorganized, but not before a competitor bid and won the rights to the area.

That competitor was William Andrews Clark and his brother J. Ross Clark. The brothers formed the San Pedro, Los Angeles & Salt Lake Railroad and planned to place a stop for their railroad in the area known as Las Vegas. The valley was the perfect choice: not only did it have an abundant supply of water, it was also a halfway point between Los Angeles and Salt Lake. Clark approached Helen J. Stewart, who

owned a large ranch in the area that was once the Mormon Fort. Stewart's husband Archibald had seized the ranch in an 1882 foreclosure. Before he was shot and killed in a gunfight in 1884, he managed to turn the site into a large ranch that stretched almost two thousand acres. Clark met with Stewart and told her of his intentions to bring his railroad to the valley. Stewart was pleased and in 1892 sold Clark the rights to 1,840 acres of the ranch for fifty-five thousand dollars.

Clark hired a surveyor and divided the east side of the ranch into thirty-eight identical three-hundred-by-four-hundred-foot blocks, forming the Las Vegas town site. He named every one of the eighty-foot-wide streets with names of early explorers like Fremont, Carson, Bridger, and, of course, Clark—names that still hold today. Each block received a specific designation, dictating the type of business that could take place on that block. Block 20 was zoned for a library and courthouse and blocks 16 and 17 were designated for the sale and consumption of alcohol. To sell his town sites, Clark held a two-day public auction on May 15 and 16, 1905.

Clark's auction was a huge success. Almost immediately saloons, brothels, and hotels began opening in tents and makeshift wood buildings. Within the first year many places had gone out of business and even more had caught fire. However, the ones that stayed eventually converted their tents and shanties into brick and stone buildings. As Las Vegas grew, brothels moved out, saloons turned into casinos, and Fremont Street became the center of downtown life.

Much has changed since 1905; however, Fremont Street is still the center of downtown Las Vegas. It's akin to what would be Main Street in most small towns. In 1995 the street was closed to vehicle traffic and covered with a seventeen-million-dollar canopy that extends the length of more than five football fields. The canopy, which has 12.5 million LED modules, creates high-resolution images and special effects in nightly shows. Today, Fremont Street is filled with musicians, comedians, and cartoon characters all vying for tourists to place "donations" in their hats, cups, and guitar cases. Kiosks on the walkway sell everything from sunglasses to sports memorabilia. However, a walk down Fremont Street can still lead to many vintage finds—that is, if you know where to look.

Long before it became home to casinos, Fremont Street was originally populated with department stores, restaurants, an insurance agency, a market, a clothing store, a beauty parlor, several pharmacies, and a theater. While all of these businesses have long since gone, many of the buildings can still be seen to this day. One of those buildings is the El Portal Theater. When it opened on June 21, 1928, it was Las Vegas's only movie theater, showing the movies of Shirley Temple, Gary Cooper, and Carole Lombard, to name a few. It also showed plays, hosted music recitals and vaudeville shows, and held high school graduations. Even Benjamin "Bugsy" Siegel once went to the movies at the El Portal.

The seven-hundred-seat, beautifully decorated theater was also the first building in Las Vegas to get air conditioning. The lobby had a Spanish motif complete with elaborate chandeliers. The stage was ornate, and a Wurlitzer organ provided music for many of the shows. Although the theater closed in 1978, the building that once housed the theater still exists, as does the theater's sign. Today the building is home to El Portal Indian Arts & Crafts.

Vintage Spots

THE GOLDEN NUGGET: EST. 1946

One of the oldest casinos in Las Vegas, the Golden Nugget was once owned by such iconic casino moguls as Jackie Gaughan and Steve Wynn. The casino was used as the opening shot in Alfred Hitchcock's *Man from the South* and in films such as *Diamonds Are Forever, Smokin' Aces*, and *Next*. The hotel now has a shark tank adjacent to the pool.

129 Fremont St.; (702) 385-7111; goldennugget.com

SAM BOYD'S FREMONT: EST. 1956

The Fremont Hotel and Casino was designed by Wayne McAllister, who also designed the El Rancho, Desert Inn, and the Sands Hotel and Casino. McAllister also designed the famous Bob's Big Boy restaurants. When the hotel opened in 1956, it was the tallest building in the state of Nevada. In 1983 casino mogul Sam Boyd bought The Fremont as part of his casino empire.

200 Fremont St.; (702) 385-3232; fremontcasino.com

THE FOUR QUEENS: EST. 1966

When it opened, the 120-room, 20,000-square-foot casino was named after builder Ben Goffstein's four daughters: Faith, Hope, Benita, and Michele. Since then it has expanded to 690 rooms and 40,000 square feet, taking up the entire block.

202 Fremont St.; (702) 385-4011; fourqueens.com

THE PLAZA: EST. 1971

Although it is officially on Main Street, the Plaza Hotel and Casino—originally called the Union Plaza—sits right at the end of Fremont Street. The hotel and casino was a business venture that partnered two of the town's moguls: Sam Boyd and Jackie Gaughan. The casino is on the site of a train station that was built in 1940 and demolished in the 1960s to make way for the Union Plaza. The casino has been the site of many movies, including *Diamonds Are Forever, Back to the Future Part II, Cool World, Honey I Blew Up the Kid, The Stand, The Mexican, Looney Tunes: Back In Action, The Girl Next Door, The Grand,* and most recently, *The Hangover Part 3.*

1 S. Main St.; (702) 634-6575; plazahotelcasino.com

Just down the block from the El Portal was Trader Bills, a leather and Western gift shop where you could purchase leather, Indian rugs, and jewelry. The building was designed to look like an old Western trading post complete with a wooden boardwalk, which was paved over in the 1950s. While the building was made to look old, it had a large, very modern, flicker-bulb sign outside. The sign, which was in the shape of an arrow and displayed the words TRADER BILLS, pointed to the store's entrance. The building now houses the Harley-Davidson store, but the original sign still exists outside the building.

One of the most famous icons of downtown Las Vegas is a sign known as Vegas Vic. Created in 1951 by the YESCO sign company, Vic is the world's largest mechanical neon sign. Vic is a classic 1950s cowboy. He is dressed in blue jeans, a red-and-yellow checkered shirt, a red bandana, a cowboy hat, and boots. A hand-rolled ciga-rette dangles from Vic's mouth. When he was created, Vic was the ambassador for the Pioneer Club, welcoming guests by waving his large arm and saying, "Howdy podner! Welcome to Downtown Las Vegas, home of the Pioneer Club." Vic was voiced by Zale Hale Jr., who died December 28, 2013, at the age of eighty-seven. While the Pioneer Club closed in 1995, Vegas Vic still remains, though he got a makeover in 2000. "I've had more work done on me than Cher, lemme tell ya," Vic told a reporter of the Las Vegas Sun. In order to fit under the new canopy, the size of Vic's hat was reduced and his arm was made immobile. He also received a new shirt and was silenced—except, of course, for interviews. Now retired, Vic concen-trates largely on his home life. Vegas Vic is a married man, hitched to a much younger woman. In 1980 the Golden Goose commissioned a large neon cowgirl, who sat cross-legged above the casino. Her top leg was originally supposed to kick, but that never seemed to work. The cowgirl's name was Vegas Vickie, though she was com-monly called Sassy Sally due to her proximity to the casino of the same name.

While the canopy was being placed over Fremont Street, the forty-three-year-old Vegas Vic married Vegas Vickie, twenty-eight years his junior. The couple is positioned on either side of Fremont Street less than a block away from each other. Vickie, who now sits above a gentleman's club, is positioned next to another iconic Las Vegas sign. The Golden Goose casino opened in 1975 and while the casino is no longer there, the cowboy-hatted goose sitting atop large golden eggs is still in place, perpetually keeping Vickie company.

Walking down Fremont Street, you can't help but feel the history rising from the pavement. So much has happened since the original auction in 1905, and while Vegas tends to be a town that changes its look like people change clothes, the history is still there waiting to be discovered. Nowhere in Vegas is this truer than on Fremont Street.

HUGO'S CELLAR

202 FREMONT ST. • LAS VEGAS, NV 89101
(702) 385-4011 • HUGOSCELLAR.COM

A Rose by Any Other Name

Hugo's Cellar is, just that, a cellar. As soon as you walk down the stairs from the floor of the Four Queens Hotel and Casino into the restaurant located inside, you get the feeling you've stepped back in time. The redbrick walls and short, maybe eight-foot-high, dark wood ceiling make you feel as if you've entered a speakeasy from the 1930s. If going downstairs isn't enough, exposed beams in the ceiling add to the feeling of actually being in a cellar. But if it's a cellar, it's the most elegant cellar you've ever found yourself in. How many cellars do you know that have their own fireplace, bar, or Renaissance-style paintings in large, ornate frames hanging on the walls throughout the place? Sitting at one of the tables you can easily imagine deals being made, businesses started, and careers launched all over a glass of wine and a luxurious meal.

"It's still the same as the old days," says Richard Assalone, manager of Hugo's Cellar, speaking of the restaurant that opened in 1976. And that is by design. The dining experience at Hugo's is unlike anything you'll find in any other restaurant—gourmet or otherwise. First of all, every woman who descends the stairs is given a long-stemmed red rose before being seated. The rose, in fact, is a theme carried—sometimes subtly, sometimes not so much—throughout the cellar. Roses show up in molded butter, light sconces on the walls, decorative glass on the bar, and on the menu itself. But a rose is just the beginning of the first-class service diners receive.

Hugo's is quite possibly the last restaurant in Las Vegas that offers table service. If you're not familiar with table service, you don't know what you're missing. Table service is just what the name implies—you are served a good portion of your meal at the table. This doesn't mean you are passed plates of food; it means your plates are prepared right in front of you. If, for example, you order Hugo's Hot Rock Specialty for Two as an appetizer, the captain will come to your table with a hot granite slab on which you'll find sizzling medallions of filet, marinated ahi tuna, a breast of chicken, and shrimp. Combined with caramelized shallots and a trio of dipping sauces, it is a truly unique experience.

Just as your appetizer is finished, a salad cart arrives. This isn't a cart filled with premade salads requiring you to point to the one you want. This is a cart which has the fixings the waiter needs to make your very own individual salad. After the waiter fills a bowl with hand-torn romaine lettuce, you are given the choice of toppings. These aren't your typical cucumber, radish, and Cheddar cheese options. Oh no, you get to choose from pine nuts, tomatoes, mushrooms, artichoke hearts and hearts of palm, chunks of blue cheese, croutons, and bay shrimp. Once you choose your toppings, you select the dressing of your choice, and the entire mixture is tossed and served on a chilled plate. When's the last time you had a salad made directly at your table?

For dinner you get to choose from a selection of steaks, including rib eye, New York strip, several different filets, and Hugo's Renowned, Slow Roast Prime Rib. If steak isn't your thing, you might prefer duck roasted with licorice spices and herbs, flambéed—with actual fire—at your table. Or maybe you'd rather have a rack of lamb or veal served as a fourteen-ounce charbroiled chop. You can also get that veal Marsala style or Oscar style—which is sautéed and topped with white asparagus and a leg of king crab all covered with a béarnaise sauce. If chicken is more to your liking, you might order Hugo's Chicken, which is a breast stuffed with sun-dried tomato pesto and served in a roasted garlic sauce. If that's not enough to whet your appetite, you might want to try raspberry chicken or chicken champignon—a pan-roasted breast stuffed with morel, shiitake, and portobello mushrooms.

Of course, if seafood is more to your liking, you can choose Chilean sea bass, ahi tuna, salmon, shrimp, and several different styles of lobster, including Queen's Lobster, which is medallions of lobster sautéed with garlic, Chablis, red peppers, mushrooms, and sun-dried tomatoes. You can also get Alaskan king crab legs, jumbo sea scallops, or Mediterranean-style scampi. Once your meal is completed,

dessert—Cherries Jubilee or Bananas Foster—is served old-style, at the table. If neither of these sound as delectable as they are, you can always go with the chocolate-dipped fruit and bowl of whipped cream.

Hugo's Cellar is a culinary treat known to both locals and tourists. "There's not many people in Las Vegas who haven't eaten here," says Richard. That's because people know a deal when they see one. Sure Hugo's is the type of place that makes you feel you should be in a fancy dress, suit, or at least a nice pair of slacks and a button-up shirt, but it's also more of a value than you might expect from a gourmet restaurant. That's because included with every meal is bottled water, warm bread, an intermezzo of fruit sorbet, that wonderful table-tossed salad, fresh vegetables, and your choice of garlic whipped potatoes, red potatoes with parsley, or wild rice. Combine all this with some of the most amazing customer service you're bound to find anywhere and you have an old-style spot worthy of the title "vintage."

This is probably why Hugo's has received the Award of Excellence from *Wine Spectator*, been named Best Gourmet Restaurant by the *Las Vegas Review Journal*, and called the Best Old School Restaurant by *Seven* magazine. "You're not gonna please everyone," says Richard, "but you can sure try."

HUSH PUPPY RESTAURANT

7185 W. CHARLESTON BLVD. • LAS VEGAS, NV 89117

(702) 363-5988 • THEHUSHPUPPY.COM

The Boss Is in the Kitchen

Come to Las Vegas and you expect to find shrimp cocktails, steaks, pasta, and even seafood, but what you don't expect to find is fried green tomatoes, catfish, seafood gumbo, sweet tea, frog legs, alligator tail, and hush puppies. But that is exactly what you'll find at one of the oldest dining establishments in Las Vegas: The Hush Puppy Restaurant. Called simply Hush Puppies by locals, this restaurant, which offers Southern-style cooking, has made Las Vegas its home since 1975. And while Southern cooking is not so easy to find in Las Vegas, what really makes this restaurant unique is how it got started.

"It took me twelve months to get financing," says owner Charlie Ghormley. "I went to every bank in town three times and every bank said to come back on Tuesday." When Tuesday came around, Charlie would go back to the bank, only to be turned down. He did this over and over again until he finally got a bank to say yes. One of the things that may have made the bankers a bit hesitant was that Charlie wasn't a restaurateur; in fact, Charlie wasn't even a chef—he was a lineman.

Charlie started his work career at a very young age. At only fourteen, he was already working in his home state of Arkansas as a laborer for the power company, which was laying power lines. He would eventually become a lineman—the person who climbs the poles and installs the power lines—a job that took him from Arkansas to towns all over the United States. "Before I got the job as a lineman, I had a set of cleats that I used to climb the pole outside our home," says Charlie. "I chewed up that pole pretty good." Charlie's path in life eventually brought him a wife and kids. Tired of moving his family all over the country, he decided to set down roots in Las Vegas. But now he needed a job, so instead of working for someone else, Charlie decided to work for himself. "I had to find something I could do and not compete with someone else," says Charlie. What he decided on was a restaurant that featured Southern cooking.

This meant Charlie not only needed to learn how to run a restaurant, he had to learn how to cook too. "In the beginning I did everything," says Charlie. "I didn't know how to do any of it. I learned along the way." Charlie traveled around the South until he found people who knew how to cook catfish and then bugged them until they agreed to show him how it was done. He also got people to help him find the best fish. "When we started there were no catfish farmers," Charlie explains. He eventually found a fish supplier who would deliver to Las Vegas and in September of 1975, he opened the doors for business.

"I stood outside the front doors and begged cars to come in," Charlie says. When that didn't work he tried another tactic. "I went on TV and they showed me cooking. That was all it took." Since then the Hush Puppy Restaurant hasn't done any advertising. They haven't had to. Charlie's goal, even from the very beginning, was to make his

guests feel as comfortable as possible in his restaurant. "I tried to meet everyone that came in the building," he says. That Southern-style feeling, combined with a home-cooked meal, has kept people coming back year after year.

Along the way, Charlie and the Hush Puppy Restaurant have made some very notable friends. Wayne Newton, Slim Pickens, Jerry Lee Lewis, and Colonel Tom Parker have all been regulars in the restaurant at one time or another. Former President Jimmy Carter even ate there once. The Hush Puppy Restaurant has perfected their catfish, serving close to one hundred thousand pounds of it every year. When Sammy Davis Jr. performed in Las Vegas, he had a standing order for Charlie's catfish, which had to be delivered to his room. Even when he was out of town he would order catfish. A couple of times Charlie had to meet Sammy's people at the airport and deliver the fish, which would then be flown to Sammy, wherever he was.

At eighty-two, Charlie is no longer in the kitchen. That baton has been passed to his son Roger, who can often be found mixing up a batch of seafood gumbo, which he learned to make by going to Louisiana and eating. "Everything in the gumbo is fresh," says Roger. "I don't open a single can for any of it." As the restaurant grew so too did the menu. "Many of our recipes have just developed over time," says Roger. One of those recipes is their green tomato relish, which they can themselves and sell at the restaurant.

At one point Charlie expanded the restaurant, opening another on the other side of town, as well as in California, Arizona, and Texas. While the businesses were doing well, Charlie found that running out-of-state businesses required a great deal of time and he eventually sold the restaurants in Texas, California, and Arizona, keeping the two in Las Vegas.

In the South, catfish restaurants could always be found down by the river, and being inside Hush Puppies you get the feeling that's exactly where you are. The walls are mainly weathered wood, with worn paint in colors of red, white, blue, green, and even pink. The wood expertly gives the restaurant the appearance of having been constructed from whatever spare wood could be found. Diners can choose from many different eating areas, some more private than others. In some areas the weathered wood has been replaced with weathered brick, which just adds to the ambience. Hand-painted

Vintage Spot
CHICAGO DOGS: EST. 1982

Located in an old A & W Root Beer building, Chicago Dogs has been serving hot dogs Chicago-style for nearly thirty years. People come in for the food and don't leave disappointed. Have yours Chicago-style with mustard, onions, bright green relish, tomatoes, sports peppers, a pickle spear, and a shake of celery salt on a poppyseed bun. You'll be screaming, "Go Cubs!"

1078 N. Rancho Dr.; (702) 647-3647

signs hang on the walls advertising oysters, fresh seafood, and other fresh delicacies. The signs rest next to folksy paintings of birds, fish, and alligators. The decor is very bayou, but also a little Polynesian.

While Charlie may have had trouble getting the bankers to back him initially, he's lasted long enough to have the last laugh. Not only has he been in business for close to forty years, the restaurant he started has received a Zagat rating and has been twice voted Best of Las Vegas Seafood by the readers of the *Las Vegas Review Journal*. So, you may ask, why name a restaurant Hush Puppy? Well, you'd probably have to be from the South to understand that one. As the sign on the wall in the restaurant says, "A long time ago . . . way down south . . . folks would roll up corn meal, fry it in deep fat, and throw it to the baying hounds to keep them quiet." Nowadays they throw hush puppies to their guests.

JESSE'S BARBER SHOP

2491 E. TROPICANA AVE. • LAS VEGAS, NV 89121

(702) 898-0400

Shave and a Haircut

t's hard to imagine Mayberry without a glasses-clad Floyd, dressed in slacks and a clean white smock, placing a thin strip of paper between his customer's neck and shirt collar before covering him in a sheetlike cloth as he sat back in the chair to get a trim and, most likely, a shave. And yet, this little slice of Americana is fading into history. That is, of course, unless you go to Jesse's Barber Shop, one of the few places left in Las Vegas where you can still get a shave and a haircut, although it'll cost you a little more than two bits.

Jesse's Barber Shop looks exactly like what you'd expect a barbershop to look like. There are four barber stations along the wall, each complete with a 1960s-era, two-tone Koken barber chair, a sink, barber supplies, and a large mirror. Tall glass jars sit on the long white counter behind the chairs at each station. The jars, which house the combs each barber uses, are filled with a blue liquid and covered with metal lids. The floor is a black-and-white checkerboard.

Metal chairs with well-used padded seats are provided for waiting customers. The chairs are positioned against the opposite wall, facing the barbers and those customers sitting in the barber chairs. Resting in the corner is a television that plays old episodes of *Bonanza, The Big Valley*, and, appropriately, the *Andy Griffith Show*. Magazines are also provided for customers who aren't either watching TV or engaging the barbers in conversation. About the only thing Jesse's is missing is a real old-fashioned barber pole on the outside of the store. Instead, there is an image of a barber pole attached to the window and a simple sign on the door that says BARBER SHOP.

Jesse J. Griffith Jr. first came to Las Vegas in 1956 when he was stationed at Nellis Air Force Base, working as a weapons mechanic. When he left the service in 1960 he returned home to West Virginia where he worked for $1.25 an hour changing oil and greasing cars. However, greasing cars for a living was not in Jesse's future. Life had other plans—including one that Jesse had never considered. But marriage often brings with it new opportunities, as Jesse would soon find out. "I married into a barber family," Jesse says. His father-in-law was a barber and it was he who talked Jesse into going to barber college.

While at barber college in Arkansas, Jesse and his wife lived in a one-room apartment over a garage. After he graduated in 1961, Jesse, his wife, his father, and six brothers all came back to Las Vegas where Jesse found a job at a little casino on Third and Ogden. It was 1963 and barbershops were still common in many Las Vegas casinos. It was while working at that job that Jesse signed a contract to open his own place at a new strip mall that was being built outside of town. It was a gamble that he would have to make work because that same day, when he returned to his job and word got out of what he had done, he got fired.

Jesse opened his first shop in January of 1965 at Tropicana and Paradise. When the rent became too high, he sold the shop and moved to his current location at Tropicana and Eastern, where he has been for eighteen years. "You stay in a place longer than you think you do when you get to thinking about it," says Jesse.

Jesse's place hasn't changed much since its opening in 1965. Jesse has no website or Facebook page and he doesn't advertise in newspapers or magazines. The barber chairs are the same ones he opened with—although some have been refurbished a bit. He still has the four barber stations, along with his own, more private, station toward the back of the shop. Instead of worrying about the latest trends, Jesse has chosen to stick to the traditional, concentrating instead on the quality of his service. Online reviews of the shop are routinely positive. "If you're looking for a true, classic, traditional barbershop, you need look no farther," reports Roger S. on Yelp. "After just a couple visits, Jesse's Barber Shop has become my go-to place for a quality cut for both my son and I," writes Joe W., on the same site.

Jesse has both new customers and customers who have been around for a while, although the new ones are getting harder and harder to come by and the industry is dying out. "You just can't find good young barbers," says Jesse, who in the '60s was considered one of the best flat-top barbers in Vegas—back when he was getting two dollars a cut. Jesse's replacements aren't coming. Instead of going to barber college, people are now going to beauty school or learning to cut the fancy haircuts that bring in more money. It's hard to work for fourteen dollars a cut when you can demand thirty-five dollars or more at a salon.

If you ask him, Jesse will admit that the worst part of his job is losing his clientele. "The hardest part of the job is when you get that phone call that one of your regulars has passed away," says Jesse, recalling a recent incident when he received a phone call from the wife of a customer who had passed. The man had been a longtime customer of Jesse's and even though he had moved out of town, he would drive back to Vegas just to get his hair cut by Jesse.

While the American tradition of a shave and a haircut may be fading into the past, the seventy-seven-year-old Jesse has no plans of retirement. "I can't sit home and do nothing," he says. "If I sold the place, I'd just be working for someone else."

THE LITTLE CHURCH
OF THE WEST

4617 S. LAS VEGAS BLVD. • LAS VEGAS, NV 89119
(702) 739-7971 • LITTLECHURCHLV.COM

The Original Wedding Chapel

*L*ong before Las Vegas became known as the Wedding Capital of the World, one lone wedding chapel started it all on what would eventually be the Las Vegas Strip. When R. A. Griffith came to town in 1941, the area that is now filled with hundreds of thousands of hotel rooms, slots machines, and table games was a vast desert in the middle of nowhere. Griffith owned a chain of 475 movie theaters and was looking to repeat his success with a chain of hotels. When Griffith saw the success enjoyed by Tom Hull's El Rancho, he decided Las Vegas was the best place to start his chain. Griffith had his eye on a thirty-five-acre parcel of land, about a mile south of the El Rancho, on which stood the 91 Club—formerly the Pair-O-Dice. The club was owned by an ex-Los Angeles police captain named Guy McAfee, who was willing to let the place go for a mere thousand dollars an acre.

Instead of opening a simple hotel, Griffith set his sights on opening a resort. He commissioned his nephew, architect William Moore, to design and supervise the construction. The resort, which Griffith called the Last Frontier, was given a Western theme. The hotel rooms were designed bungalow-style, meaning they were one-story rooms all connected in a row. To counteract the effects of the desert heat, Griffith had close to four thousand trees, plants, and shrubs planted around the property. He and his engineering staff also developed an ingenious method of cooling the bungalows. Tunnels were dug under the rooms and used to circulate cold water. The water was

then passed through pipes installed in the walls of the rooms, keeping them cool. Bugsy Siegel would later use this technique to cool the rooms of his Flamingo Hotel.

The main building was designed to resemble a lodge. It had high ceilings and a fireplace that sat in the center, its chimney running right up through the roof. Griffith brought in Navajo workers from New Mexico who set stone from nearby Red Rock. He also transferred the forty-foot mahogany Gay Nineties Bar from the famous Block 16 Arizona Club that was once located in downtown Las Vegas but had closed. Bar stools were carved to look like saddles. Façades were added to the building and arranged to give the appearance of a street from an old Western town.

The Last Frontier was the first to have what would eventually become a Las Vegas staple, a wedding chapel. Located in the Last Frontier Village was the Little Church of the West—often called the Hitching Post. The little church looks almost exactly the same now as it did when it was built in 1942. It's constructed almost entirely of California redwood, an exact replica of a pitched-roof church built in a pioneer town. The walls of the one-room church are made of alternating narrow and wide redwood pieces that extend from the floor to the ceiling. Wood benches serving as pews are positioned at angles on either side of the church and a wood organ rests at the front near the preacher's podium.

Like most Old West–style churches, the Little Church of the West has a steeple with an actual bell. However, instead of the steeple being on the church, it's placed adjacent, but still connected to the church. According to popular legend, the bell in the steeple came from the church in St. Thomas, Nevada—the town that was flooded to create Lake Mead. Not only was the Little Church of the West the first wedding chapel located on a Las Vegas resort, it has the distinction of being the first and only freestanding wedding chapel on the Las Vegas Strip. This is because a Las Vegas ordinance now prevents the construction of freestanding wedding chapels on the Strip.

During the '50s and '60s, the hotel and casino passed through many different hands. All this time the church remained under the same management, though it was moved from the north side of the property to the south side in 1954. It would remain for another quarter century, performing weddings on a daily basis. It was while in that location that its future owner, a teenage Greg Smith, frequently drove by the little church. "You'd drive down the Strip, you'd see the little picturesque church sitting there and happy people," says Greg who got his start in the wedding business as a photographer. "It's kind of ironic that I ended up making a career out of it."

In 1979 the church was slated for demolition to make room for the first mall on the Strip. At the time it was operated by Merle Richards, who had started working as a photographer at the church shortly after World War II. "The people who were running the chapel asked if they could keep it," says Daniel Vallance, marketing director for the Little Church of the West. In a move uncommon in Las Vegas, Richards was given the green light and he moved his church south, down the Strip, to the site of the old Hacienda. Four years later, in 1983, Smith bought the church from Richards. However, as Las Vegas is prone to do, the Hacienda too was slated for demolition to make way for the modern and upscale Mandalay Bay, putting the Little Church of the West once again in danger of the wrecking ball.

But Smith would have none of it. He wasn't about to let the church, which was so steeped in Las Vegas history, fade into the sunset. After all, besides the hundreds of thousands of weddings performed for locals and tourists over the years, the church had played host to such notable couples as Richard Gere and Cindy Crawford, Angelina Jolie and Billy Bob Thornton, and Redd Foxx and Ha Ka Cho. In addition, celebrities such as Robert Goulet, Zsa Zsa Gabor, Judy Garland, Mickey Rooney, and Betty Grable have all tied the knot at the Little Church of the West. Even Elvis Presley and Ann Margret got married at the church—on film in *Viva Las Vegas,* of course—and it's the church's actual bell that can be heard in the background at the end of the movie.

In Smith's eyes, there was only one thing to do—move the church. So, once again, and for the final time (for now), Smith moved the Little Church of the West directly across the street, not far from the equally famous WELCOME TO LAS VEGAS sign, where it sits to this day. "We're on the Strip, but we're far enough away that it's not crazy, and we have a lot of parking here," says Greg. While weddings and wedding chapels are a mainstay in Las Vegas, the Little Church of the West stands apart. "We do one ceremony at a time," says Daniel. "We organize things so different parties don't see each other. We keep it more personal that way." Personal service is, and has always been, the tradition of the Little Church of the West, which in 1992 was placed on the National Register of Historic Places. Of course, having been around since 1942, the little church has seen many faces, most of which still live in the valley. Perhaps Daniel puts it best when he says, "Everybody knows somebody who was married at the Little Church of the West."

A LITTLE WHITE CHAPEL

1301 S. LAS VEGAS BLVD. • LAS VEGAS, NV 89104

(702) 382-5943 • ALITTLEWHITECHAPEL.COM

Here Comes the Bride

For sixty dollars you can get a marriage license in Las Vegas (unless you pay by credit card; then it's sixty-five). With the license in hand, you are free to get married, that same day if you like, in any of the city's 192 wedding chapels. Many of these chapels are inside major casinos—the MGM, the Venetian, the Bellagio, Mandalay Bay. Still more are stand-alone buildings located right on the legendary Las Vegas Boulevard. None, however, is more famous than A Little White Chapel.

The aptly named chapel is as unique as its owner Charolette Richards, who acquired it in a closed bid in the late 1960s after the original owners were unable to keep it running. When the chapel came up for sale, Richards, along with many other hopefuls, placed her bid. There was only one problem. "I had no money," she says with a coy smile. But money was not about to stand in the way of Cupid's arrows. Once all the bids were received, Richards' came out the highest and, as you might expect, was accepted; now she had a problem.

"I had to somehow come up with the fifty-thousand-dollar deposit," she says. At the time Richards, who is known affectionately as Ms. Charolette by her staff, owned a flower shop called Flowers by Charolette on the grounds of the Last Frontier—a thirty-five-acre resort built by Texas movie theater mogul R. A. Griffith on the Las Vegas Strip. Griffith opened what was probably the first wedding chapel on the strip—the Little Church of the West—and Ms. Charolette ran the flower shop right next door.

One of her regular visitors in the shop was Bert "Wingy" Grover, a casino host at Caesars Palace. Grover, who was rumored to be "connected," got his birdlike moniker due to a deformed arm. The casino host, who had a custom of wearing small carnations in his lapel, was a frequent visitor to Ms. Charolette's flower shop and the two struck up a friendship. Grover had once told Ms. Charolette that if she ever needed anything, all she had to do was ask, and now that time had come. So she screwed up her courage and went to see Grover. His response was to take her to the bank.

Once the papers were signed Ms. Charolette and her four small boys moved into the four-room building. "I lived here in the chapel," she explains. "For six months I did everything myself until I was able to pay back the money I borrowed." Which she did, in full. At the time the "chapel" was one small room in an equally small home. The house itself was located on the outskirts of Las Vegas. It was surrounded by a field of lush green grass and adorned with beautiful trees.

Las Vegas has since grown up around the little home that housed a wedding chapel. The green grass has been replaced by gray concrete and the trees by many varied buildings containing pawn shops, motels, bail bond services, tattoo parlors, strip clubs, and yes, even other wedding chapels. Through it all, however, Ms. Charolette and A Little White Chapel have not only been able to survive, but thrive and expand. While the home that houses the original chapel still exists, Ms. Charolette has managed to buy up several of the buildings around her, buildings which now house her offices, other chapels, flower shops, and dress shops. She has also installed a large gazebo on the grounds and a drive-up Tunnel of Love. "We could perform seven ceremonies at once if we needed to," she boasts with a wide smile.

Just how many weddings have been performed at the chapel is a bit of a mystery. When pressed for a number Ms. Charolette simply says "a lot." An ordained minister herself, she recently performed fifty ceremonies on the *Steve Harvey* show. "When they introduced me, they said I'd performed 1.7 million weddings. I thought to myself, 'Where'd they get that number?'" The truth is, it could be 1.7 million. But it could also be more or it could be less. Ms. Charolette doesn't really know. If pressed for a daily number, however, she'll tell you the twenty-four-hour chapel averages around thirty weddings a day,

although that number is likely low. There is one day, though, that sticks clearly in her mind. That day was July 7, 2007, and it was her busiest day. "We performed close to five hundred weddings on that day," she recalls. That large number is likely attributed to seven being considered a lucky number, especially in Las Vegas.

Couples who visit the chapel have their choice of five rooms in which to be wed. The original kitchen is now a chapel decorated to resemble a beautiful green garden, complete with waterfall. Ms. Charolette calls it the Jordan room because it is the room where Michael Jordan got married. In fact, the chapel has played host to the weddings of many famous people including Rita Hayworth and Dick Haymes, Joan Collins and Peter Holmes, Sarah Michelle Gellar and Freddie Prinze Jr., and Bruce Willis and Demi Moore—a wedding Ms. Charolette officiated herself.

Like the building, the room where ceremonies originally took place still exists, only now it's twice the size. Once Ms. Charolette grew tired of living in the chapel she purchased a home a short distance away. She then expanded the original wedding room into what was once her living room. The room is entered through its original white leaded-glass doors. The walls inside are covered with wedding-bow-decorated wallpaper. Two sets of white pews with red velvet

Vintage Spot
WEE KIRK O' THE HEATHER WEDDING CHAPEL: EST. 1940

Scottish for "Little Chapel of the Lucky Flowers," the Wee Kirk o' the Heather wedding chapel has been marrying couples for more than seventy years, making it Las Vegas's oldest continually operating wedding chapel. The chapel has been in business so long that many couples who married there originally have returned forty or fifty years later to renew their vows.

231 Las Vegas Blvd.; (702) 382-9830; weekirk.com

cushions rest on either side of the room, creating an aisle down which the bride and groom travel to the preacher. A sliding stained-glass door leads to a garden area at the right of the chapel. A window on the left houses three stained-glass pieces shaped in the easily recognizable point of a chapel. Two of the pieces are roses, while the center piece contains two white kissing doves silhouetted by a large heart.

For those people with a wedding emergency or who just want to get the wedding done as quickly and easily as possible, A Little White Chapel offers drive-up weddings in their Tunnel of Love. "Drive up in your car, motorcycle, bicycle, or even skates and our friendly wedding coordinators will make your dream come true," the recorded phone message promises. "We were the first chapel anywhere to offer a drive-up wedding ceremony," says Ms. Charolette.

While a drive-up wedding may be convenient, it does beg the question why anyone would want such a ceremony. That question may best be answered by Pierce and Kristie Harvey, who were married by Ms. Charolette in a drive-up ceremony on February 18, 2014. The couple—who grew up across the street from each other—had lost touch over the years and had recently reconnected through social media. Once rejoined, they married, but when Pierce tried to use his military status to get a home loan, the recent wedding blocked their path. "We had the wedding annulled so Pierce could get the loan," says Kristie. But once the loan went through, the couple wasted no time. They drove right back to Las Vegas as quickly as possible to wed anew, only this time they stayed in their car. Instead of the fancy glitz and glamor, they pulled up to a small sliding window, on the other side of which was Ms. Charolette ready and waiting. "We just wanted it to be quick and easy," Kristie said. "We already had our ceremony."

Oddly enough the drive-up wedding was created because of a nuisance Ms. Charolette was being forced to endure. "At that time the marriage bureau was open twenty-four hours a day," she says. "When people were looking to get married right away, the bureau sent them to my house." Couples would wake up Ms. Charolette, who would then marry them in her driveway. "I got tired of getting no sleep," she says, "so I opened the drive-up wedding."

You might wonder what effect owning a wedding chapel has had on Ms. Charolette. "I'm around happiness and love every day," she says. "I love every minute of that portion of the business. I stand with people at their new beginnings. What could be better?" What indeed.

LOST VEGAS ANTIQUES

625 S. LAS VEGAS BLVD. • LAS VEGAS, NV 89101
(702) 382-1882 • LOSTVEGAS.VPWEB.COM

What Was Once Lost Is Now Found

When you first walk up to Lost Vegas Antiques, you can't help but wonder what you've gotten yourself into. Standing in front of the bright yellow building is a full-size pirate, complete with sword and pistol; a balding waiter wearing a white apron; and a pink swimsuit-clad, brown-haired bathing beauty standing next to an old-fashioned English telephone booth, all under a bright blue canopy with large pink letters that read LOST VEGAS ANTIQUES.

Painted on the exterior walls are various road signs, cartoon characters, and the four lads from Liverpool. Signs posted on the windows advertise COLLECTABLES, VINTAGE VEGAS MEMORABILIA, and one sign that simply reads, ELVIS. Below an antique Pepsi Cola sign sits a larger Coca-Cola sign. Next to the cola signs is one advertising Ted's Root Beer and another with a cartoon character of Superman. Other signs hang down from the canopy advertising CURIOSITY SHOP COLLECTABLES, OLD COINS & TOKENS, CASINO CHIPS, SODAS AND ICE TEA, and BOTTLED WATER, which sells for one dollar.

On top of the roof are the front ends of two cars, a Volkswagen Beetle and some other unidentifiable car. Each vehicle, which is the same color red, has inexplicably been cut just behind the front wheels—the remainder of the car completely missing. A large red die rests behind the sawed-off Beetle and an old light-up Coca-Cola sign with the word ANTIQUES above the Coca-Cola logo is attached to the front of the canopy. Flags from America and other countries adorn the top of the building running down the side. While the outside of

the building may have you wondering, stepping inside does nothing to curtail those worries, because the inside of the building is just as eclectic as the outside.

Lost Vegas Antiques got its start in 1989, though it has been in various locations during that time. It is owned and operated by Rich Burgel, the self-proclaimed boss, bouncer, and buyer. Lost Vegas got its start as part of the Las Vegas Historical Gambling Museum at the Tropicana Hotel and later the Lost Vegas Gambling Museum on Fremont Street. If you are looking for vintage Las Vegas, you need go no farther than this intriguing antiques store.

Inside these walls you'll find the most complete assortment of old Las Vegas collectables that have ever been assembled in one place. Lost Vegas is probably one of the only places left in Las Vegas—outside of a museum—where you can find an actual plate from the ill-fated Moulin Rouge Hotel and Casino. The Moulin Rouge, which opened in 1955, was the first casino in Las Vegas to cater entirely to the African-American community. The casino fell into bankruptcy and closed within six months of its opening, and even though several attempts were made to rescue the property, it eventually fell to an unceremonious end when it mysteriously burned to the ground in 2003 after sitting vacant for many years. However, before it went under, it was once owned by Sarann Knight Preddy, the first African-American woman to hold a gaming license.

Lost Vegas Antiques is also the only place where you can find such items as an employee manual from the Sands. These manuals were given to new employees of the hotel and covered everything from how to dress, to how employees were expected to conduct themselves while working on the casino floor. If employee manuals aren't your thing, how about a flyer advertising the room rates for the Sands Hotel & Casino, giving the property an address of Highway 91—long before the road from California became the Las Vegas Strip.

One display is dedicated entirely to the early days of the Flamingo Hotel and Casino. In this particular display case you'll find glasses, ashtrays, dice, chips, cards, bowls, and plates, all decorated with pink flamingos. There is a decanter shaped like a large pink flamingo, as well as coasters, cocktail napkins, postcards, envelopes, bingo cards, swizzle sticks, and a room-service menu. There are champagne glasses, whiskey glasses, and mixed-drink glasses all with the pink flamingo logo. They even have shot glasses with Bugsy's mug plastered right on them. At the back of the display rests a photo of Siegel, taken right after he was killed in the California bungalow of his girlfriend Virginia Hill.

Only at Lost Vegas Antiques will you find an actual room key to the Sahara Hotel. Not one of those plastic cards they give you now, but an actual metal, slide-inside-a-keyhole room key, complete with a tag that guarantees its return to the hotel if dropped in the mail. There are chips from almost every casino in town, including many that no longer exist, such as the Sands, the El Rancho, the Landmark, the Thunderbird, and the Mint.

The best part about Lost Vegas Antiques is that the more you look, the more you find. You want a hanger from the El Rancho? They've got it. How about a swizzle stick from your favorite 1950s or 1960s casino? They've got that too. What if you want a paper cup from the Boulder Club, the Desert Inn, or the Pioneer Hotel & Gambling Hall? Yup, they've got those as well. In fact, there's hardly anything you won't find inside these walls. They have a large collection of vintage Las Vegas photos along with postcards from almost every casino that is, or has been, in Las Vegas. They even have the tokens that were used in casinos in place of silver dollars.

"We love to talk about collections," says Rich, sitting behind the large counter. "And anything vintage." Rich's love for vintage shows in every part of the store. Where else can you find a dice clock from the old Hacienda, a miniature brass shovel commemorating the ground-breaking of the Dunes Hotel, or the ducat bag from that casino? At Lost Vegas Antiques you can find ashtrays from the El Rancho, the Sands, and the Hotel Last Frontier. You can also find matchbooks from almost every casino, including the Moulin Rouge. Lost Vegas Antiques is also likely the only place outside of eBay where you can buy a copy of Jack Cortez's weekly entertainment magazine called *Fabulous Las Vegas*, which ran from 1948 well into the 1950s.

Rich also loves to barter. Everything has a price marked, but none of those are set in stone. All you have to do is shoot him an offer and he'll shoot back a counteroffer until you both get to where you want to be. Just about everything that was ever made in Las Vegas has probably, at one time or another, passed through the doors of Lost Vegas Antiques, and if you want to spend several hours lost in a vintage time warp this is where you should come, because if you can't find vintage Vegas here, you won't find it anywhere.

THE MIDWAY AT CIRCUS CIRCUS

2880 S. LAS VEGAS BLVD. • LAS VEGAS, NV 89109
(702) 734-0410 • CIRCUSCIRCUS.COM

The Circus Has Come to Town

In the face of gambling, drinking, and other adult-oriented entertainment, one casino has defiantly maintained a family-friendly atmosphere, one where mom, dad, and all the kids can enjoy cotton candy, hot dogs, carnival games, and circus acts, all while staying in one of the oldest remaining casinos on the strip. Circus Circus was the brainchild of Jay Sarno, who in 1966 opened the seven-hundred-room Caesars Palace to critical acclaim. With his first casino showing a profit, Sarno wanted to do something that had never been done. He wanted to create a place where adults could go to gamble and children could go to play. The theme for his new casino—the circus. Sarno figured he could get the best circus acts in the country, reasoning that performers would be more than happy to live in the same place all year round.

The casino, which was to be called Circus Circus, was designed by architect Homer Rissman to look like a giant pink and white, oval-shaped circus tent. Gambling was to be located at the bottom of the tent, while carnival games were to be placed on the second floor. A trapeze was to be situated at the top of the tent, where the circus acts would perform. When adults tired of being with their children on the second floor, they could get to the casino floor through the traditional method of going down stairs, or they could choose to slide down a fireman's pole or go down a giant slide. Sarno even brought in a baby elephant named Tanya who was trained to pull the handle of an oversized slot machine with her trunk.

Sarno told the *Las Vegas Review Journal* in 1968, "The customer will be confronted with jugglers, fortune tellers, trapeze and high-wire acts operating right over the gambling area. We have signed the finest circus acts in the world." He also promised "a spirit of fun and gaiety." The hotel opened on October 18, 1968. Sarno had hired Clarence Hoffman—a veteran of the Chicago Opera—to act as ring-master. What Sarno hadn't done was give Hoffman a script. About an hour before the casino was about to open, Hoffman went to Sarno and asked Sarno what he wanted him to say as ringmaster. Sarno told him, "You'll think of something." At the same time, another little disaster was taking place. To celebrate the opening, fifty thousand balloons had been anchored to the roof by a layer of netting. As a camera helicopter was making a practice run over the building, the helicopter's rotors created a draft that tore through the netting, set-ting the balloons prematurely free. However, in true circus fashion, the show went on.

As people lined up twelve deep anxiously awaiting the open-ing celebrations, Hoffman stepped up to the microphone and said, "Lights." He was immediately hit by four spotlights. He then thought to himself, "What would a ringmaster say?" He quickly arrived at, "Ladies and gentlemen, introducing Circus Circus, the most exciting casino in the world!" The crowd erupted in cheers.

Vintage Spot
THE FOUNTAINS AT CAESARS PALACE: EST. 1966

On the last day of 1967 Evel Knievel made one of his most famous jumps—over the fountains at Caesars Palace. While Knievel easily cleared the fountains, his landing was not as flawless. He crashed on the landing ramp, suffering a concussion, fracturing his pelvis, and breaking his leg, wrist, and both ankles. The landing was shown over and over again on television for many years. Knievel's son Robbie would successfully jump the same fountains twenty-two years later.
3570 S. Las Vegas Blvd.; (702) 731-7110; caesarspalace.com

The first circus act to perform that night was the Flying Palacinis. The acts, which were supposed to end at 2 a.m., lasted well into the morning, finally ending at 6 a.m. due to performer fatigue. Sarno's gamble had worked. His idea was a complete hit, and just as he suspected, circus performers were dying to sign up. "Everyone wanted to work for him," Jay's daughter September once said, "because it was the first chance they'd had to live in one place and have normal lives."

That same theme has endured for more than forty years and Circus Circus is still the only casino on the strip that still has an attached KOA Campground. Moms, dads, and kids can all still enjoy free circus acts in the Circus Theater on the Midway located on the second floor of the casino. Families can sit on stadium-style benches and watch clowns, trapeze artists, jugglers, and acrobats from Russia, South America, China, and the Ukraine. Once you enter the Midway, you find yourself in a carnival atmosphere—just like one you might find in any small Midwestern town. Barkers, bright flashing lights, and large prizes hanging at each carnival booth entice families to lay down a sawbuck or two in the hopes of winning a prize.

Here you can race clowns, horses, knights, or even camels by throwing a small red ball into colored holes that make your clown, horse, knight, or camel move forward along a straight line. How fast the clown, horse, knight, or camel moves depends on the color of the hole. If rolling balls into holes isn't your game, you can play Knock Down. In this game players shoot balls with an air-compression gun at clown faces. Knock down three clowns in a row and you win a prize: a stuffed animal. You get six balls for fifty cents.

If you prefer, you can try your luck at tossing a Wiffle ball into an angled basket. If the ball stays in, you win a stuffed animal. In another game you throw a small foam ball into a reduced-size basketball rim. For only one dollar you get two balls and, if you get both balls in the basket, you win a prize—another stuffed animal. If pitching is your thing, you can throw a beanbag at three blocks positioned to the back of a pedestal. You get one beanbag for two dollars or three for five dollars. If you knock all three blocks off the pedestal with one throw, you win—you guessed it—a stuffed animal.

If pounding is more your style, you might enjoy Chicken in a Pot. In this game you place a stuffed chicken on a launching pad and slam the launcher with a mallet. You get two chickens for a dollar and if either chicken lands in the pot, you win. The more chickens you get in the pot, the bigger your prize. If you want a more traditional game, you can try landing a Ping-Pong ball into floating cups that are moving counterclockwise. If your Ping-Pong ball lands in the clear cup—and the majority of the cups are clear—you get three more balls. Landing in a red cup gets you a small prize, yellow a medium prize, and getting your Ping-Pong ball in a blue cup gets you the largest prize, which, by the way is a stuffed animal.

If you need a break from playing carnival games and are ready for a snack, you can go to the Horse-Around Snack Bar. There you can get a glass of refreshing lemonade, a soda, or an Icee and choose from a hot dog, cheese dog, or a chili-cheese dog. Of course no trip to the carnival would be complete without cotton candy, and you can get that at the Horse-Around as well. Once your food arrives, you take a seat at a carousel horse as the entire snack bar slowly rotates in a circle.

When a day filled with carnival games, cotton candy, clowns, and trapeze artists comes to an end, even if the prize walked away with was a bit smaller than the one hanging in the booth, mom, dad, and the kids all have big smiles on their faces. And even though Las Vegas bills itself as an adult playground, there is still one place where the family that stays together can play together.

MJ CHRISTENSEN DIAMONDS

10400 S. EASTERN AVE. • HENDERSON, NV 89052

(702) 763-8096 • MJCHRISTENSEN.COM

A Diamond in the Rough

*L*as Vegas is often called the wedding capital of the world, and it's easy to see why when close to 130,000 couples get married here every year. Weddings in this town are performed both day and night. You can get married in a chapel, a casino, on stage, or even in the great outdoors. Heck, you can even get married in your car. For this reason, you might expect to find all sorts of jewelry stores in Las Vegas ready and eager to sell you a ring. Well, you certainly can and that's the problem. "Sometimes we're seen as being akin to used car salesmen," says Cliff Miller, who with his wife Darlene owns MJ Christensen Diamonds. But that's not what MJ Christensen is about. That's not what kept the jewelry store in business for three quarters of a century.

Marcus Joy, the "MJ" of MJ Christensen, first came to Las Vegas in 1927 as a watch inspector for the Union Pacific Railroad. Running a railroad is all about time—when a train arrives at the station, when it leaves the station, when it arrives at its destination—and it's important that everyone's timepieces are in sync. It was MJ's job to make sure all the clocks and watches were just that. He did this job for a couple of years, but eventually moved back to Salt Lake City with his wife Hazel, his son Vern, and his daughter Anna—who was named after his mother. While in Salt Lake City, MJ and Hazel had two more sons—Carl and Paul—and a daughter, Adele. MJ tried his hand at selling insurance, but found it wasn't to his liking, so he eventually made his way back to Las Vegas, where in 1939 he opened MJ Christensen Diamonds on the corner of First and Fremont in downtown Las Vegas.

Even from the start, MJ did business a little differently than other jewelers. He didn't cheat his clients, he didn't price items above their worth, and he wasn't a high-pressure salesman. Simply put, he was honest. "Everyone describes him as an angel on earth," says Cliff. And it was that honesty that allowed MJ to open seven more stores in the Vegas valley. "By 1968, MJ dominated 80 percent of the jewelry in Las Vegas," explains Cliff. MJ wasn't just known to the residents of Las Vegas; he had some very famous clients as well. Movie stars William Powell and Myrna Loy bought jewelry from him, as did Liberace—a Las Vegas resident and one of its most famous entertainers.

MJ's reputation took him well beyond his jewelry store. It took him all the way to the Nevada State Assembly where he served from 1952 to 1960. During that time he also served as president of the Chamber of Commerce in 1954 and the president of the Better Business Bureau in 1956. Seven years after he left the state assembly, he was elected to the state senate. MJ continued to expand his business, opening stores in the 1970s and '80s, until his death in 1987 at the age of eighty-eight. After MJ's death, his son Vern took over the family business, running it the same way his father had run it before him, until 2000 when at seventy-eight Vern decided to get out of the jewelry business. Unfortunately no one in the Christensen family wanted to take over the business, so Vern had no choice but to sell.

Enter Cliff and Darlene Miller, two Georgians with over forty years experience in the jewelry business. Both Cliff and Darlene are registered graduate gemologists with the Gemological Institute of America, and are members of the American Gem Society—something only one in twenty American jewelers can claim. When MJ Christensen became available, it caught the couple's attention. "I heard the business was for sale," says Cliff. "So I did some investigating." They found MJ Christensen Diamonds attractive for one main reason—its business philosophy and ethics fit perfectly with the ones Cliff and Darlene had already put in place. "We're an ethical company," explains Cliff. This means, much like MJ himself, Cliff and Darlene don't cheat their clients, don't price items above their worth, and aren't high-pressure salespeople. In fact, they're anything but that.

If you're looking to buy a diamond ring, but don't know anything about diamonds, Cliff, Darlene, or one of their salespeople will be happy to give you a lesson . . . or two, even if you don't buy from them. And their knowledge doesn't just end with diamonds. It's gems and jewelry of all kinds. In fact, it's not at all uncommon for people to bring in jewelry they bought at other stores or in other countries to see if they got a good deal or were, well, you know . . . cheated. Heck, you can even bring in your family heirlooms and they'll tell you what they're worth. "It's fun going through people's treasures," admits Cliff.

But even an ethical jewelry business can't fight a struggling economy, so when Las Vegas, like the rest of the United States, slipped into a crippling recession, Cliff and Darlene were forced to reduce their staff and their inventory, and close some of their stores. Now they're down to two locations—one on the west side of town and one on the east side of town. And while they may have been forced to make some tough business decisions, one thing never changed—their commitment to honesty, integrity, craftsmanship, and excellent guest service. "We approach the jewelry business to establish relationships," Cliff emphasizes. "Our staff isn't just here to sell."

Unlike Vern, Cliff and Darlene may not have to worry about what happens to the business when they decide to retire. This is because both their children are part of the equation. Rusty, who himself is a gemologist, is in charge of all the custom work—something he is very good at—and their daughter is the company's model. Like MJ, Cliff and Darlene take their commitment to the Las Vegas community seriously. They are involved with organizations such as Opportunity Village, Best Buddies, United Way of Southern Nevada, Dress for Success, Diamond Empowerment Fund, the Diamond Development Initiative, and BeadForLife. "We believe in giving back," explains Cliff. "Back where I came from jewelers are respected." Sometimes they're respected out in the West as well. It is clear that Cliff and Darlene have done MJ proud. It's easy to imagine him looking down from above, smiling and giving his approval, knowing his business and his name are both in good hands.

THE MOB MUSEUM

300 E. STEWART AVE. • LAS VEGAS, NV 89101

(702) 229-2734 • THEMOBMUSEUM.ORG

An Offer You Shouldn't Refuse

In 1933 when the US Post Office and Federal Courthouse opened its doors, the four-story building was the tallest in town. "By Las Vegas standards this building is old," says Geoff Schumacher, director of content development for the Mob Museum. The museum, which is officially known as the National Museum of Organized Crime and Law Enforcement, opened in 2012 after then Mayor Oscar Goodman made a deal that would pave the way. The old courthouse had been decommissioned several years earlier and was sitting vacant. Goodman, who is most well known for defending the likes of Meyer Lansky, Frank Rosenthal, and Anthony Spilotro, officially purchased the building for one dollar from the General Services Administration with the condition that it be refurbished and used as a museum.

Way back in 1999 Goodman had an idea. "It dawned on me, 'What differentiates us from any other city in the world as far as where we came from?'" says Goodman. "And I said, 'The mob.'" And with that realization the Mob Museum was born. "They brought in top-notch companies to build the museum," says Geoff. One of those was the husband-and-wife team of Dennis and Kathy Barrie who were tasked with designing the museum. They spent a great deal of time creating interactive exhibits and filling them with the best pieces of mobster and law-enforcement memorabilia they could find. When the couple was done, they had created one of the foremost educational experiences Las Vegas has to offer.

You should be warned that the Mob Museum isn't your typical stuffy, don't-touch-anything type of museum. The Mob Museum

proves, as Geoff likes to say, that "museums can be entertaining and educational." This is because the museum doesn't just present displays and exhibits. Sure, there are plenty of vintage items on display just as you might expect in a museum, but there are also many ways to get involved in the history. After you pay the fee to enter, you take an elevator to the third floor. The elevator, which is original to the building, even has one of those fancy dials on the outside above the door that indicates the floor the elevator is on. When you get off the elevator you are "chosen" to participate in an actual lineup, and by participate I mean you are one of the people in the lineup, standing behind the glass, turning left or right as requested by the police. At this point you get to decide for yourself which side of the law you prefer and walk down that path.

One of the detail-oriented exhibits is set up to look like the Arizona Club. The saloon, which was visited by the likes of Wyatt Earp, was a Las Vegas staple from almost the beginning of the town in 1905. The saloon started as a wood building, but as it became one of the most popular places on block 16, it was converted to brick. It was also given a rich wood front that was decorated with fancy leaded glass and ornate metal. Inside the exhibit, the saloon is designed to look much like it would have in the early 1900s. Photos and history hang on the walls and it is in this room where you learn quite a bit about life in early Las Vegas. A gambling table is set up inside the saloon, and you can sit down and bet against fellow museumgoers in an interactive gambling game. The more you known about Las Vegas history the more virtual coins you can win. (Hint: the answers are on the walls of the saloon.) Of course, the game is just for fun and no coins—virtual or otherwise—go home with you.

The second floor of the museum contains two exhibits most noteworthy to Las Vegas. The first is a large and original courthouse. "A lot of people were sent to jail in that courthouse," says Geoff. And while that is most certainly true, the courthouse is most famous for hosting hearings that tried to root out and disrupt organized crime. By 1950 the mob had developed a strong foothold in America—one they were not willing to relinquish. Virtual nobodies had become prosperous running bootleg alcohol, gambling, and prostitution. Long before the days of text messages, tweets, and selfies, the mob had gained a far-reaching influence right under the collective nose of the unsuspecting American public. All that changed when a mob kingpin was found dead in a Democratic clubhouse. A bright light had been shined on the mob and the United States government had had enough.

Enter a Senator from Tennessee. Estes Kefauver, who had his eyes set on a little white cottage in Washington D.C., was put in charge of a committee to find, indict, and convict mobsters. In 1950 Kefauver's traveling show came to Las Vegas and the Federal courthouse. On the second floor of the Mob Museum is the actual courtroom in which members and suspected members of organized crime were grilled by Kefauver and his committee. The hearings moved from town to town, and when it was all said and done, over eight hundred witnesses had testified; however, few indictments or arrests were made and Kefauver never got to see that cottage from the inside. In the museum you can sit in the actual courthouse on the original benches and listen to a multiscreen presentation about the hearings and their inevitable results.

The other exhibit on the second floor shows Las Vegas during the time it was under mob influence and deemed an "open city," meaning no one syndicate dominated Las Vegas. As the museum states, the open-city designation made Las Vegas "an enticing destination for mobsters nationwide." This exhibit, more than any other, celebrates what many would consider to be the heyday of Las Vegas. Here you can find a large collection of items from such Las Vegas icons as the Flamingo Hotel, the Desert Inn, and the Hotel Last Frontier. Inside a glass display case is a photo of mobster Meyer Lansky surveying Las Vegas, a powder blue jacket worn by the staff at the Desert Inn, and a leather briefcase—with an elaborate gambling scene tooled into the leather—that belonged to mob front man Moe Dalitz.

In the same display case you can also find a photo of the famous El Rancho Dice Girls and a pennant celebrating Las Vegas as the atomic testing grounds. There is also a photo of Dalitz playing golf with comedian Bob Hope near a photo of a topless Josephine Baker, who once performed at the Hotel Last Frontier. Above the photos are various gentlemen's magazines such as *After Hours*, *Sir*, and *Cabaret*, the latter of which asked on its cover, "Do Gangsters Run Las Vegas?"

On the wall opposite the display case is a large screen that shows photos and videos of Las Vegas, along with music from the likes of Dean Martin. An interactive table in front of the screen tells the story of the Las Vegas Strip. The exhibit also has old slot machines, various cheating devices, and remnants of the Sands Hotel and Casino's chips that were embedded into the floor during a remodel that moved the famous Copa Room. Another interactive display even lets you "spot the scam." You can also find a copy of the infamous black book—so named for the color of its cover—which provided the names and photos of all persons "excluded" from casinos.

In a town whose main source of entertainment is gambling, the Mob Museum is a welcome and refreshing change. "If you spend a couple of hours at the Mob Museum, not only will you be educated, you will be enlightened about American history," says Geoff. There is so much inside that you can easily spend an entire afternoon watching the videos, experiencing the interactive displays, and even, if you so choose, taking the Blood Oath to become a made man—or, you know, made woman. As Geoff likes to say, "You're not going to be bored at the Mob Museum." So if you're thinking about skipping the museum, fuhgeddaboudit.

NATIONAL ATOMIC TESTING MUSEUM

755 E. FLAMINGO RD. • LAS VEGAS, NV 89119

(702) 794-5151 • NATIONALATOMICTESTINGMUSEUM.ORG

Freeing the Atomic Genie

On August 9, 1945, the United States dropped the second of two nuclear bombs on Japan, resulting in their surrender five days later. The dropping of the bomb may have taken Japan out of World War II, but it also ushered in an unprecedented period in American history that would be known as the Atomic Age. This is the story told by the National Atomic Testing Museum.

The museum originally opened in 2005 as the Atomic Testing Museum. However, on January 3, 2012, the museum got an upgrade. On that date it became one of only thirty-six museums to be designated as national museums. "We went from telling the story of the Nevada test site to telling the nation's story of atomic testing," says Karen Green, the museum's curator. "We're the only national museum in Las Vegas."

The Atomic Age was a unique time in Las Vegas's history. It all started on January 27, 1951, at 5 a.m. when residents of Las Vegas awoke to an unexplained rumble, which they only later found out was an atomic explosion. Knowing what happened to the unfortunate souls in both Hiroshima and Nagasaki, it's little wonder the residents of Las Vegas were more than a bit upset about not being told of the impending test. "The atomic bomb! No one asked us what we thought about it," wrote Georgia Lewis in her book *The Way it Was: Diary of a Pioneer Las Vegas Woman*. "Everyone is in an uproar, for none of our officials know anything about this."

The Atomic Energy Commission, established five years earlier in 1946, had tried to keep the first aboveground test of an atomic bomb a secret, but when you explode a bomb of that magnitude out in the open, it's a little hard to keep people from finding out. If the rumbling ground didn't clue them in, or the mushroom-shaped cloud in the distance, the blast's bright light—which could be seen as far away as San Francisco and Los Angeles—certainly gave it away. In fact, it was a truck driver who saw the explosion as he was coming down the hill toward Stateline, Nevada, that broke the news. "He got into Jean and he very nicely called the *Review-Journal*, and we got an eyewitness account of the blast," recalled *Las Vegas Review-Journal* editor John F. Cahlan.

Once the word got out, Las Vegas businesses had two choices—either fight against the testing, or exploit them. They chose the latter. A spot was set up on nearby Mount Charleston, which provided a perfect view of the blasts. Hotels organized picnics, bakeries created mushroom-cloud cupcakes, and restaurants added atomic burgers and atomic cocktails to their menus. The Las Vegas Chamber of Commerce even produced a calendar of scheduled blasts for tourists.

When they decided they could no longer hide the blasts from the public, the government established a vantage point, called News Nob, on a rocky cliff that overlooked the site. Dignitaries of the news, including Cahlan, Walter Cronkite, and Bob Considine of the *New York Times*, were invited to view the blasts from News Nob.

The test site broadcasted public-radio notifications of scheduled tests, warning people not to be in high places, such as ladders, during the test. Blasts were commonplace. "The people in the casinos would be gambling and so forth, and they'd see the big flash of light," says Cahlan. When the flash was over they'd return to their games, saying, "Well, there goes another one." On November 12, 1951, Las Vegas made the cover of *Life* magazine with a photo of an atomic cloud visible behind the neon signs of the Pioneer and Las Vegas Clubs. The resourceful executives of the Pioneer Club turned the photograph into a postcard. The Desert Inn followed by making its own mushroom-cloud postcard.

But probably the most memorable tribute to the atomic era came in the form of a woman covered in a cotton front piece shaped like a mushroom cloud. The Sands Hotel Casino held a competition crowning Miss Atomic Bomb of 1957. Copa Room showgirl Lee Merlin, a blond-haired beauty, became an enduring symbol of the era with

nothing more than outstretched arms and a mushroom-shaped cotton cloud covering her midsection.

Between 1951 and 1992, 928 tests were performed; 100 of those tests were aboveground. When you are in the museum you quickly gain an understanding of just how incredibly amazing and horrifying that time was. After we dropped the bombs on Japan, the nuclear race was on and with it a Pandora's box of potential outcomes—not all of which had happy, Disney-style futuristic endings.

The museum takes the visitor on a tour through the Atomic Age. One of the exhibits is about Mercury, Nevada—the test site basecamp established off a dirt road once known as the Mercury Highway. The basecamp was the place where workers at the test site worked, ate, slept, and entertained themselves. At the museum you can see the office of Frank Rogers, the first site manager. It is set up just the way it would have looked in 1954. If you listen closely, you can even hear news reports related to the atomic bomb coming over Rogers's office radio. A small theater just to the left of Rogers's office explains the atom—protons, electrons, and neutrons—in an old cartoon informational show from the '50s. The show was done in a manner intended to make people feel good—and safe—about atomic energy.

All areas of the Atomic Age are covered in the museum, which has many interactive displays, videos, and voice recordings, as well as QR codes that can be used with a smartphone to get even more information. One display shows the atomic bomb's effect on popular culture. Here you'll find Atomic Fireball candy, a space-age repeating cap pistol, atomic tape made from asbestos, and a box of Kix cereal the prize inside of which was an Atomic Bomb Ring—an actual plastic replica of the bomb attached to a ring small enough to fit on a child's finger. You can also find an old *Superboy* comic in which Superboy is asked to swallow two "new chemicals" so scientists can observe the explosion in his stomach through an x-ray.

One of the most unique exhibits is the Ground Zero Theater, where you experience just what it was like to witness the testing of a nuclear weapon. You sit inside a concrete-reinforced bunker looking into a small window at the front. A voice countdown signals the blast. After detonation all is silent. The first thing you see is a bright, overpowering light and then a cloud of dust rushing toward the window. As the ground begins to rumble and shake and the cloud of dust overtakes you, it's easy to understand the power involved in such a blast.

Another unique display shows mannequins in a 1950s fallout shelter. The mother, father, and child are frozen in a perpetual state of readiness as they wait for the impending blast. J. C. Penney, who donated mannequins for experimental testing, published before-and-after photos of their mannequins in the local paper back in the '50s, in an attempt to get residents involved in civil defense. A television in the shelter shows the films created to get people ready for a possible nuclear attack on US soil. It is both fascinating and unnerving.

As you leave the mannequins in their fallout shelter, you enter a tunnel that takes you down to the area that deals with underground testing. In this area of the museum you can become a test director and set off your own atomic bomb. In the Innovations Gallery, you come face-to-face with an actual B-53 thermonuclear weapon—well, not an actual armed weapon, but one that was used for training purposes. Here you find that the bomb could be detonated in a number of ways including a retarded air burst using the bomb's five parachutes. It is also in this gallery that you hear from the people who worked at the test site. Men and women who were tasked with creating an implement of destruction so powerful, so metamorphic, it was like releasing a genie from a bottle. As they tell you their stories, you gain a solemn understanding of both the burden they bore and the sense of patriotism they felt.

While the eight-thousand-square-foot museum is almost hidden on Flamingo Road, not that far from the Strip, it doesn't stop the museum from getting local, national, and international visitors. The museum is a treasure trove of information relating to one of the most exciting and horrific times in our nation's history. "This is very unique," says Karen about the museum. "You're not going to find this anywhere else."

THE NEON MUSEUM

770 N. LAS VEGAS BLVD. • LAS VEGAS, NV 89101

(702) 387-6366 • NEONMUSEUM.ORG

Lighting Up the Night Sky

When you pull up to the Neon Museum, it can be hard to remember that it is, in fact, a museum. This is because it's not really like any museum you've ever visited. There aren't any exhibits to speak of, and to enjoy the collection, you have to go outside. In fact, a portion of the collection isn't even at the museum, it's on the busiest street in Las Vegas. However, in all the right ways, the Neon Museum is definitely a museum, one that is unique in its collection of vintage Las Vegas history.

As soon as you arrive, you see multiple colors and shapes peeking at you from behind a fenced-in area, known as the Neon Boneyard. The shapes, of course, are the signs, and they beckon you to come inside. You may not know what's waiting for you, but you know you want to find out. If you're looking for a taste of Las Vegas history, you won't be disappointed. It abounds at the Neon Museum from the moment you enter the iconic visitors' center. The building, which served as the lobby for the La Concha Motel, is iconic for many reasons, but most notably for its shape. Formed as a joining of three sweeping arches, it looks strangely like something you might find on the head of the Flying Nun.

The building is actually a perfect example of "Googie" architecture. Established in the 1940s, Googie is influenced by the space age, or what Americans envisioned the space age to be. Think George Jetson, jet packs, the space race, and atomic energy. The building is also iconic because it was designed by Paul Revere Williams, an African-American architect who went on to design many Las Vegas

landmarks, such as the Guardian Angel Cathedral. The building was built in 1961, but by 2005 the La Concha had closed and the famous lobby was scheduled for demolition. Luckily, the Doumani family—who owned the La Concha, the El Morocco, and for a time the Tropicana—donated the building to the museum. In 2007 it was reassembled and offices were added on behind.

The office building itself is a silent wink and nod to its historic counterpart. The tiles on the outside of the office building are meant to replicate the tile that once surrounded La Concha's pool. Windows go from ground to ceiling and are designed to look like the sliding glass doors that were on each room of the motel. Sunshades above each window are meant to replicate La Concha's balconies.

Of course, the whole reason for the Neon Museum is the signs. Neon signs have a rich history in Las Vegas. In fact, Vegas is almost as well known for its neon signs as it is for showgirls, slot machines, the Rat Pack, the mob, or ninety-nine-cent shrimp cocktails. Las Vegas's most iconic symbol isn't a jumpsuit-clad Elvis, a casino chip, or even a dice clock. It's a neon sign, created in 1959, that simply says, WELCOME TO LAS VEGAS.

Las Vegas is a town of opulence, in more ways than one. The only thing that changes is how Las Vegas chooses to demonstrate that opulence. In the '50s, '60s, and '70s, it did it with signs. At one time, a trip down Las Vegas Boulevard, famously known as the Strip, involved flashing lights, bright colors, and large, bigger-than-life signs. Every casino had one. The Hacienda had an incandescent bulb-filled palomino horse complete with a neon rider dressed in a green Spanish-style suit, flat-brimmed hat, boots, and oversized spurs. The Stardust had a sign meant to celebrate the Atomic Age, complete with cosmic lettering, planets, and stars. Circus Circus had a huge red-haired, neon, red-nosed clown in a striped, pointed hat, and ruffled collar, holding a spinning lollipop bigger than the clown's own face. The Silver Slipper had a silver, bulb-adorned, glitter-covered, high-heeled woman's shoe with a gold bow. The shoe would not only light up at night, flashing brightly, but also rotate—something that once upon a time drove millionaire Howard Hughes insane.

And it wasn't just the casinos that had these attention-grabbing signs. Outside almost every downtown business was a neon sign, an incandescent sign, or a combination of the two. The Lucky Cuss

Motel, Chief Hotel Court, and the Normandie Motel all had bright, flashy signs. Dot's Flowers had a neon sign. So too did Atomic Liquors, Charleston Auto Parts, and the El Sombrero Restaurant. The Bow and Arrow Motel's sign shot a neon arrow. While these signs had only one purpose—to draw your attention—the competition to create the best, most outrageous sign spurred a new type of art.

In the 1980s, as signs transformed into super-sized movie screens, the old-fashioned Las Vegas standard was in peril. It was at this time that members of the community, those interested in Las Vegas's culture, recognized the city's rapid growth might spell doom for the neon sign. In 1996 the city of Las Vegas, in conjunction with the Allied Arts Council, founded a nonprofit organization with the intent of saving, collecting, restoring and, eventually, exhibiting Las Vegas's most precious signs. That organization became the Neon Museum and the land on which the signs were stored became the Neon Boneyard.

Signs make their way to the Neon Boneyard largely through donations. However, donating the sign isn't enough. It still has to be moved from its current location to the boneyard, and that often involves a crane, a large truck, and a great deal of money. In some cases the sign has to stay in its current location for years before enough money is raised for the sign to find its way to its new home at the boneyard.

Just because a sign makes it to the boneyard doesn't mean it gets restored. In some cases collection is enough. "We recognize the value of the sign as an object of art whether or not it gets restored," says Danielle Kelly, the museum's executive director. This means the museum isn't only interested in signs that can be restored, it's interested in saving an art form. Of course, a lucky few do get a second chance at life, but that chance comes with a high price tag. It can cost anywhere from $12,000 to $180,000 to restore a sign. The Neon Museum is, above all, a museum, and being a museum, their task is to restore the sign, not simply make it work again. "We don't rebuild," says Danielle. "We restore." This may mean finding someone who knows the technique that was used to build the sign originally or training someone to learn that technique.

You might think any sign lucky enough to be restored is displayed on the grounds of the museum, but you'd be wrong. Restored signs light anew along Las Vegas Boulevard in an outdoor gallery. The first sign to receive this honor was the Hacienda's Horse and Rider sign, also known as the Hacienda Caballero sign. If you're wondering why this sign, which was created by the Young Electric Sign Company in 1967, became the chosen one, Danielle has the answer. "It's the first sign we had," she says. The sign was restored through a generous donation and placed at the intersection of Fremont Street and Las Vegas Boulevard, where it sits to this day.

What started with one sign is now many, lighting up downtown Las Vegas with good old-fashioned neon. Along with the Hacienda Caballero, you can find signs such as Binion's Horseshoe, the Silver Slipper, the Bow and Arrow Motel, and Society Cleaners, with the Golden Inn and the Apache Motel next on the restoration list. In 2009 this portion of the strip became designated a National Scenic Byway by the US Department of Transportation. It is one of only three urban byways in the United States. "We feel what makes this a beautiful drive is the signs," says Danielle proudly.

Not to be outdone, the Neon Museum has its own neon sign— well, sort of. The sign is actually next to the museum in a park that is owned by the city, but is in the custody of the museum. There sits a modern sign with a vintage flair. Each letter of the word "neon" is a typographical reference to an historic Las Vegas sign. The "n" is from the Golden Nugget, the "e" from Caesars Palace, the "o" from Binion's Horseshoe, and the final "n" is from the Desert Inn. Parts of the sign also reference the Stardust and the Sands, but you'll have to visit the museum to find out how.

In 2002 the Neon Museum became separate from the city, but its mission has remained the same. Along with the boneyard and out-door gallery, there is also a living museum, which is a collection of signs around the valley that are still in use today. To be part of the living museum, a sign owner has to promise to notify the museum if they plan to take down the sign and to give the museum first dibs to buy it. Of course, while preserving Las Vegas's past is important to Danielle, she would prefer the signs stay up and operational. "The last thing we want is for a sign to come down," she explains. "We want it doing its job: bringing in customers to the business and lighting up the night sky."

THE OMELET HOUSE

2160 W. CHARLESTON BLVD. • LAS VEGAS, NV 89102

(702) 384-6868 • OMLETHOUSE.NET

Sometimes You Gotta Break a Few Eggs

*I*f you're going to call yourself the Omelet House, you'd better be prepared to deliver upon that proclamation. You'd better have the best dang omelets in the city and they'd better be worth the trip. Well, the Omelet House is certainly worthy of the name, because not only does it serve the best omelets in the city, it serves the largest. This isn't your typical three-egg omelet. Oh no. This is a six-egg omelet, one that's not for the faint of heart. It's the kind of omelet you have to invite your family, friends, and possibly neighbors to help you finish. You've heard of a two-fisted drinker? At the Omelet House you'd better be a two-forked eater.

The Omelet House started in 1979 and since then it has been the go-to breakfast place for locals and tourists lucky enough to ask a local where to eat breakfast. "People come here to make their deals over breakfast," says owner Kevin Mills. "What's better than sitting down, relaxing, and having a little breakfast while you talk business? We became the place to do that after Poppa Gar's closed," Kevin says, speaking of the longtime Las Vegas breakfast destination that closed in 1998. Not only was the restaurant the only place in town where you could get quail eggs for breakfast, it was the place where governors, assemblymen, senators, and the Las Vegas business elite all gathered to talk turkey.

But while the Omelet House may have taken over Poppa Gar's business, this restaurant has its own distinct vibe. The original location on Charleston Boulevard is easy to miss if you don't know what you're looking for, but it's worth the effort to hunt down. The restaurant is hidden toward the back of an older shopping plaza. If you go in the morning, especially on the weekend, the parking lot will be full. Once you get there, simply look for the large stained-glass window above the door that reads GARDEN EATERY and step inside.

Once you pass the front doors you find a restaurant with a decor that has changed little since its opening in 1979. The walls, which are made of mostly wood paneling, are decorated with all manner of knickknacks, country-style signs, cookie jars, and salt and pepper shakers. Wire baskets filled with faux houseplants hang from the ceiling among the Tiffany-style stained-glass light fixtures. A large mural of a mountain scene complete with a soaring eagle, pine trees, and a crystal clear lake is painted on the back wall. The restaurant is cozy, charming, and more than a little welcoming.

"We built this place on a shoestring budget," says Kevin, who got his start in the kitchen of Battista Locatelli—owner of the iconic Battista's Hole in the Wall. When his family started the restaurant it was confined to a small room that is now referred to as the Garden Room. In 1988 they took over the area next to them, calling it the New Room—a name it still holds to this day. Under his family's guidance the Omelet House quickly became one of the most popular breakfast

spots in town. "People were lining up outside the door on Saturday and Sunday waiting for a table to open," explains Kevin. It didn't take long for him to realize an expansion was in order. "I'm from Vegas, so I don't normally gamble, but I took a gamble and opened more space," he says. It was a gamble that paid off. While more space meant more expenses, it also meant the Omelet House could now seat more people, making waiting outside a thing of the past.

All you have to do is eat at the Omelet House once and you understand why all those people were eagerly waiting outside. Sure, they have the traditional breakfast items—homemade corned beef hash, eggs Benedict, waffles, pancakes, French toast, chicken-fried steak—but what really sets them apart is their namesake: their omelets. The Omelet House puts just about anything in their omelets that can be put in an omelet. There are thirty-four different choices that range from just cheese to the Kitchen Sink, which, as the name implies, has it all. If you want asparagus, mushrooms, and Cheddar cheese on your omelet, then the Spartacus—a Kirk Douglas special—is the omelet for you. How about avocado, tomato, and Cheddar cheese? Then try the Green Hornet. Or, if you prefer, one of your party can order the Porky Pig while the other orders the Petunia Pig—Porky's girlfriend.

If chili is more to your likin' try the Cowboy Special, which is filled with the Omelet House's homemade chili, Cheddar cheese, and onions. As the menu says, "Folks come from far & near for this one!" However, if you want to go vintage, try the Bugsy Siegel. This six-egg omelet is filled with tender chunks of roast beef in an Italian red sauce with sour cream and Jack cheese. It's "an omelet you can't refuse." If you like seafood, try the Shrimp Boat or the Loch Ness Monster, although you're not allowed to take photos of that last one.

The Omelet House's menu is about as inviting as the food is good. Clever little puns are hidden amongst the menu items and it's fun to seek them out while you're trying to decide what to eat or waiting for your meal after you've ordered. But if you do the latter, read fast because you won't be waiting long. Food comes quick; it's good and it's inexpensive. In fact, the most expensive omelet on the menu will cost you a mere $11.69. That is, unless you order the $69 Flatlanders Special, but I wouldn't recommend it unless you want an omelet filled with raw liver, organically grown black jelly beans, and grunion lips—assuming, of course, the grunions are running.

Vintage Spot
EGG WORKS: EST. 1988

Want a Bloody Mary with your breakfast? Better head to Egg Works, a locals' favorite for over twenty years. Egg Works is famous for its oversized portions, breakfast potatoes, and hot banana bread. Rachael Ray even went there on an episode of *Rachael Ray's Vacation*. A little Vegas secret—the owners of Egg Works also own the Egg & I and the Cracked Egg, both in Las Vegas.

2490 E. Sunset Rd.; (702) 873-3447; theeggworks.com

The Omelet House is truly a family-run restaurant. Both Kevin's daughters work there, as does his wife and mother-in-law. Of course, Kevin hires others to help out. But don't just think you're going to work there and earn a quick buck, 'cause if you're young and want to work at the Omelet House, Kevin has one very strict rule. "You gotta stay in school," says Jake, one of Kevin's servers. You see, Kevin is not only a family man, he is a Las Vegan—born and raised—with deep roots in his community and in Nevada. His grandfather was from a small town called Bullfrog, Nevada, and he grew up with the children of Jay Sarno, who was responsible for both Caesars Palace and Circus Circus. Kevin—whose mother put him through private school working as a cocktail goddess at Caesars Palace—remembers when Las Vegas was still a small town, when business was done on a handshake, and you knew your neighbors. Which is probably why he hosts a regular event called the Las Vegas Legends Breakfast, where the people who made Las Vegas what it is today—the last standard bearers of a noble history—meet, tell stories, and have a bit of breakfast. "I'm pleased to rub elbows with the people who started this city," says Kevin. The breakfast is his way of honoring the past, something he takes very seriously.

PAMPLEMOUSSE LE RESTAURANT

400 E. SAHARA AVE. • LAS VEGAS, NV 89104

(702) 733-2066 • PAMPLEMOUSSERESTAURANT.COM

C'est Si Bon

ecause I'm French" is the response you'll get from Georges La Forge if you ask him why he opened a French restaurant in Las Vegas. It seems like an obvious answer, but you have to remember that in 1976 when Georges opened his gourmet restaurant, which specializes in French provincial food, the town had a heavy mob influence and French food wasn't exactly what people expected when they came here. But Georges didn't worry about what people would expect. Instead, he decided to concentrate on giving the public the unexpected and it has worked for nearly forty years.

Georges's restaurant chops are well established in Las Vegas. He initially came here as a young man—one who didn't speak English— working as a busboy at the Riviera. He eventually made his way up the ladder, working in such notable casinos as Caesars, the Dunes, MGM, and the Desert Inn, where he became the maître d'. It was there that Georges met and developed a friendship with singer Bobby Darin, famous for such songs as "Splish Splash," "Dream Lover," and "Mack the Knife." One night Georges and Darin were enjoying a meal at the Skillet Room—a locals' hangout—when Darin made Georges an offer. "I've always dreamt of opening a small French restaurant," he told Georges.

But while Darin wanted to own the restaurant, he had no delusions of being able to operate it. He understood the place had to be run by someone who knew what they were doing, and that someone in Darin's mind was Georges. Darin told Georges he'd fund the restaurant if Georges ran the place. There were, of course, a couple of

stipulations. The first was that the restaurant had to be located in Beverly Hills, California, and the second was what the restaurant would be called. Darin, who spoke fluent French, loved the French word for grapefruit. "He wanted to write a song called 'Pamplemousse,'" says Georges. "It was his favorite French word."

Unfortunately, Darin died in 1973, at the age of thirty-seven, due to complications of heart surgery he had undergone to fix two artificial heart valves that were installed two years earlier, so the two men never became partners. However, the dream stuck with Georges and less than three years after his friend's death, he opened a small French restaurant and named it in honor of the singer, calling it Pamplemousse Le Restaurant. Georges chose a little house, built in the 1950s, just off the Strip as the spot for his restaurant. This is why, when you enter the front doors to the Pamplemousse, you feel more like you've been invited into Georges's house than a restaurant.

Darin's dream of a small restaurant is completely fulfilled in the fact that the Pamplemousse seats only about seventy-five guests. Tables are covered in white linens. The lights are low and the walls are decorated with photos of past guests, such as Debbie Reynolds, along with framed photos of movie stars. There is an antique fireplace, a wine cellar, and support beams made of dark, rich wood that make the place feel like a French country cottage. "People take a peek inside and find it very homey," says Diana Boicheff, marketing director at Pamplemousse. "Going to an old house, to them it's something special," adds Georges.

Finding a French restaurant in Las Vegas is hard enough, but finding one that has changed little since its opening is nearly impossible. "I wanted to change it," says Georges, "but people would say, 'What are you going to change?' They don't want anything to change." Diana hits the nail on the head when she says, "People come here because there is a soul to it." That doesn't mean the decor is old and outdated. Actually, it's quite the opposite. Walking into Pamplemousse today still feels as if you're walking into Georges's home and it's a house you definitely want to be in.

Up until recently Pamplemousse didn't even have a menu. Waiters were expected to know each specialty by heart and they were expected to recite those specialties to diners. Meals changed according to the season and what George wanted to cook. "We have hundreds and hundreds of cookbooks at home," says Georges, who takes those cookbooks and uses them to stimulate his imagination. They help him come up with new items such as escargot with shallots deglazed with cognac, toasted almonds, and Roquefort cheese in a cream sauce. Which, by the way, is served on a bed of angel-hair pasta. "It's really different and people love it," says Georges. However, while Georges is open to new ideas, his emphasis is on a certain type of food, one his customers have come to expect. "A lot of our menu is traditional provincial," he says. "People come here to eat their favorites. I appreciate new ideas, but not so much the trendy."

Eating at Pamplemousse is an experience, one that takes some time. Several of the desserts have to be ordered in advance because they take around twenty-five minutes to prepare, and the meal itself can require a significant commitment of time. From the moment you are served the complimentary crudités (assorted raw vegetables) at the beginning of the meal, the traditional French onion soup gratinee with Swiss cheese, the duck breast and leg confit or rack of lamb, to the hot chocolat lava cake or chocolat soufflés at the end of the meal, you can be there for two hours or more.

The requirement of time is definitely not a deterrent in the restaurant routinely voted Las Vegas's most romantic, which is why

Pamplemousse is sold out a year in advance on every February 14. "People come here because they know they won't be bothered," says Georges with a smile, adding, "We get generations of people. Many people who dined with us when they were children, now bring their children here. We always have a lot of repeat business." In a city that routinely changes its look to meet the most current trend, it's nice to find a place that understands the appeal of Vegas the way it used to be. "We're old school," says Diana, "and that's the lure of it."

THE PEPPERMILL RESTAURANT AND FIRESIDE LOUNGE

2985 S. LAS VEGAS BLVD. • LAS VEGAS, NV 89109

(702) 735-4177 • PEPPERMILLLASVEGAS.COM

Some Things Are Better Left Unchanged

*I*n a city like Las Vegas, you'd expect one of the most well-known places to be something like a casino, showroom, or possibly the site of a mob hit. But in truth, arguably the most well-known place in Las Vegas is a little restaurant on the Strip that has been around since 1972. Step inside the Peppermill Restaurant and you quickly realize you're not in a typical Las Vegas eatery. In fact, you feel more like you've just walked into a 1960s-era lounge or casino. The swirly patterns in the carpet, just as in casinos, are designed to keep your attention upward. The mirrored ceilings are reminiscent of gaming pits before the advent of cameras, when pit bosses used to look at the reflection of the games—and the players—to make sure everything was on the up and up.

Walking into the eating area is like passing into some type of *Alice in Wonderland* psychedelic garden. The aqua, blue, and purple-padded, oversized booths are lined with purple neon lights. Tiffany-style lamps hang down over each table and fake trees and foliage adorn the areas between the tables, making you feel as if you've just stepped into some kind of bizarre purple forest. The low lighting and purple neon accents create an ambience that works perfectly.

The real draw of the Peppermill is how you're treated when you step inside this fascinating world. Close to 30 percent of the staff have been working there for ten years or more and some have been there since day one. "There are a lot of staff who have met their spouses here," says manager JoAnne Valentine, who herself has been working at the restaurant off and on since her teens. According to JoAnne, eating at the Peppermill is like eating with family. "Our regulars come here because they see the same people. We know what they eat and what they drink, and we know their secrets."

That last part is probably the most important because not only do locals and tourists alike eat at the Peppermill, so too do celebrities—especially local celebrities. In fact, famous people come here because the restaurant doesn't make a big deal about the famous people who come here. "It's possible to sit at a booth and see someone famous sitting in the booth next to you," says JoAnne. "It's fairly common." In its early days, that person may very well have been Frank Sinatra, Dean Martin, Sammy Davis Jr., or Liza Minnelli. Currently you may find Carrot Top, Guy Fieri, Floyd Mayweather, or Giada de Laurentiis.

If you go at night you're likely to see Penn Jillette, the six-foot, six-inch half of the famous Las Vegas duo Penn and Teller. Jillette, who himself talks about his love for the restaurant, is so enamored with the place that he had a replica of a booth built in his own house. "I'm always comfortable sitting and talking with Gilbert Gottfried or Paul Provenza in the Peppermill all night, so I knew I could sit all night

at this table and be very, very happy," Jillette told reporter Kimberly McGee in an interview with the *Las Vegas Sun*.

Jillette also commented on the other thing the twenty-four-hour Peppermill is most famous for: its home-style cooking. "They have big food," Jillette explains, describing the portions as "Flintstone food." "You go up there, they put the plate down and your whole car tips over." One of the best examples of this is the Western Fruit Plate. This dish—which comes piled high with an entire pineapple, two bananas, an orange, and various other fresh fruits—looks more like something Carmen Miranda would wear on her head than what you'd expect to see in a restaurant for $13.95. And if the fruit alone isn't enough for you, the plate is accompanied by an entire loaf of banana bread. If you come to eat at the Peppermill, you might first want to fast for a couple of days.

The restaurant, however, isn't the only thing that attracts people to this Las Vegas hallmark. Connected to the Peppermill, toward the back, is the Fireside Lounge, so named for the sunken, round pit that features fire dancing on glowing water. The ambience that starts in the restaurant continues in the lounge, which was named one of America's 10 Best Make-Out Bars by *Nerve* magazine. But if you plan on going to the lounge, you'd better be prepared to observe the strict dress code. "No hats, caps, visors, sweatbands, bandanas, or head coverings of any kind. NO EXCEPTIONS," exclaims the sign on the door to the entrance. Bartenders are dressed in white shirts and black slacks and servers come to you dressed in form-fitting, long, black dresses, complete with a slit up the leg. When you come here, you just feel like you should be dressed well.

Like its counterpart the Peppermill, the Fireside Lounge enjoys a bit of notoriety. A pre-Whitney-Houston Bobby Brown threw stripper-filled private parties in the lounge and Martin Scorsese used it as a backdrop for his Vegas-based movie *Casino*. The lounge was also featured in such movies as *Showgirls* and *The Cotton Club*, as well as in television shows like *The Holly Madison Show*, *MTV Spain*, and an episode of *Giada at Home*. The lounge even served as the backdrop for supermodel Heidi Klum, who once did a photo shoot there for *Marie Claire* magazine.

If you're not interested in sightseeing, you can always bring your significant other to the lounge, settle into one of the booths, and share a sixty-four-ounce Scorpion or one of the Fireside's award-winning Bloody Marys, which they make from scratch, and see what happens. As you settle into the booth it's easy to picture yourself back in the days when the mob had a strong influence in Las Vegas. A time when Tony "the Ant" Spilotro and his crew hung out at the Fireside Lounge, not only for its drinks, but because its back door provided them an easy escape route.

Regardless of why you come to the Peppermill Restaurant or the Fireside Lounge, you'll leave happy, full, and satisfied. "Everyone has a nice memory about this place," says JoAnne. And with more than forty years of practice, memories are what the Peppermill family specializes in.

PIERO'S ITALIAN CUISINE

355 CONVENTION CENTER DR. • LAS VEGAS, NV 89109

(702) 369-2305 • PIEROSCUISINE.COM

Legendary Since 1982

At one time in Las Vegas people dressed up. They put on suit jackets, fancy shirts, dark slacks, and ties. They slid into long, sleek dresses and decorated their necks with shiny stones and pearls. They dangled jewelry from their ears and fixed their hair into buns and curls and waves. After they got all dolled up, they headed into town or took the elevator into the casino to see a show or go to a restaurant. Back then shows were an event. Dinner was served, most had a two-drink minimum, and when the show was over, the stars came out into the casino to mix and mingle with the regular folk. Back then you could sit at a gaming table and rub elbows with the likes of Dean Martin, Joey Bishop, Peter Lawford, Marilyn Monroe, Humphrey Bogart, or Frank Sinatra.

Those days went away long ago when corporations began buying up casinos, consolidating properties, and changing the face of Las Vegas. Nowadays, all you need to see a show are tickets. Sure, you can get dressed up, but chances are you'll be sitting next to someone in shorts and a T-shirt that says "Got Vegas?" But if you're looking for old Las Vegas, if you long for the glamour of the old days, there's still one place left where you can be transported back in time to the Vegas of yore and, if you're lucky, rub elbows with members of the Las Vegas elite. That place is Piero's Italian Cuisine.

While Piero's is old by Vegas standards, it only goes back to 1982. Not that being in business for thirty-some years isn't quite an accomplishment, it's just that with Piero's ambience, you'd expect the restaurant to have been open since the early '50s or '60s. As soon as

you walk in the rich, dark, wooden front door, you realize you've left the twenty-first century behind and headed back to a Vegas where business was conducted over dinner and a drink. Where people, all with the middle name of "the," gathered to eat and conduct a little business. A time when people meant what they said. When your word was your bond. Old Vegas. Something Piero's understands very well.

Piero's got its start when Fred "Freddie" Glusman met Chef Piero Broglia at Broglia's restaurant on Sahara Avenue. At the time Freddie owned the Sporting House, which had a little coffee shop inside. Freddie enjoyed Chef Broglia's food and the two struck up a friendship. Freddie would bring samples of Chef Broglia's cooking to the Sporting House, hosting what he called "Piero Nights." The events became so popular the duo decided to open a restaurant together on Karen Avenue and name it after Chef Broglia. "Piero was the chef," says Evan Glusman, Freddie's son and operating partner of Piero's Italian Cuisine. "Dad was the maître d'." The restaurant was an immediate hit and it didn't take long for lines of diners, eagerly waiting for a table, to gather every night outside the door.

The partnership would change one night when Freddie decided to throw a party for Luciano Pavarotti. "We did a party for Pavarotti and it sold out almost immediately," says Freddie. Guests went to

Pavarotti's show and then came to Piero's for dinner. Two of those guests requested a special vegetarian dinner. Freddie didn't see it as a problem. "We're going to try our best to make you happy," says Evan. "If it's in our realm, we're going to do it." Chef Broglia, on the other hand, didn't see it that way. He was the chef and thought people should eat whatever he served them. When he refused to cook vegetarian fare, the founder and his chef had reached an impasse. The chef walked out. "With a little bit of encouragement from me," says Freddie. Although Chef Broglia left, he wasn't able to take his name with him—no matter how hard he tried.

Even without Piero in the kitchen, the restaurant didn't miss a beat. "I know food," says Freddie. He went out and hired Gilbert Fetaz as his executive chef and while Chef Broglia lasted only weeks, Chef Fetaz has been there since 1982. Freddie also moved the restaurant to its current, much larger location on Convention Center Drive. Piero's Italian Cuisine seems to have forgotten about time. It's as if someone walked into the luxury restaurant and froze a part of it—not its decor or menu, but its ambience. Piero's is still the place to see and be seen. In the old days Freddie used to have dinner with Sammy Davis Jr. Nowadays you can find Tiger Woods, John Travolta, or United States Representative for Nevada Rochelle "Shelley" Berkley eating at Piero's. Part of Scorsese's movie *Casino* was filmed there. Many of Piero's famous guests are immortalized in photographic form on the walls of Freddie's office—and it is a sight to behold.

If Piero's has a specialty, it's treating people well. "When you walk in the door everyone knows who you are," Freddie says. "You have a special table, most of the time, if you're a special customer." "Special customers" get their names on a table in one of the smallest, but most popular, rooms in the restaurant. Often called the VIP room, it has only ten tables. "Celebrities come here because we make sure they can eat without being bothered," says Piero's Captain Linda Kajor, who herself has worked there for twenty-five years. "And we pour the best damn drink in town," she adds with a smile. Of course, if you happen to be an ex-UNLV basketball coach by the name of Tarkanian, and if you happen to have won a national championship, you get your own entire room.

The food at Piero's is northern Italian at its best. It's the kind of food that makes you wish the meal would never end. The fresh-baked

Vintage Spots

THE SICILIAN RISTORANTE: EST. 1988

Started by Pietro and Mimma Gumina in 1988, this Italian restaurant serves all your classic Sicilian favorites like osso buco, caponata, and fettucine alla Siciliana. Eat at this restaurant and you'll understand why they say, "Dining Sicilian style is almost like making love . . . you really must take the time to enjoy it."

3520 E. Tropicana Ave.; (702) 458-2004; siciliancafe.com

RAO'S ITALIAN RESTAURANT: EST. 2006

Rao's Las Vegas is run by the same family who started the famous New York Restaurant in 1896. Located inside Caesars Palace, Rao's is a replica of the original New York ten-table restaurant, updated with additional seating and a bocce ball court in the back. Walk into this restaurant and you'll understand why they say, "You immediately smell Italy."

**Caesars Palace Drive; (702) 731-7267;
caesarspalace.com/restaurants/raos**

bread that comes to your table is truly Italian—hard crust on the outside, soft and airy on the inside. The staff works as a team, meaning you never have to wait for "your" waiter to get more water, another drink, or, well, anything. If you've never had Italian food before, you should start here, but be warned, you may never find food anywhere else that stacks up. In a land of famous-chef-owned restaurants, Piero's doesn't only stack up, it shines. The food is, in a word, spectacular!

But it didn't get that way by accident. If there is a vetting process for food, Evan has created it. "I've eaten everything on the menu," he says, "multiple times." Evan, who believes you can tell much about a restaurant by the amount of time the owners spend in the place, makes sure the food is up to Piero's high standards. "If something isn't quite right," says Evan referring to the food, "I order it ten times until its right." But he doesn't stop there. He orders it again, periodically, to make sure the quality stays the same. Which is why the food at Piero's is some of the best in Las Vegas. And while they have many old Italian favorites, they also have new creations, like the Garbage Caesar Salad, which Evan himself created. "One night I just wanted something different, so I told the chef to make me a Caesar salad and asked him to put shrimp, avocado, tomatoes, and hearts of palm in it," says Evan. They were Evan's favorites. "People began coming in and asking for 'that salad you made Evan,' so we put it on the menu," he says. It became a huge hit.

Another huge hit is the appropriately named Monkey Bar—appropriate because it's filled with Jose Bellver's paintings of chimpanzees. You may be wondering how paintings of monkeys made their way into an Italian restaurant. It's simple. "Jose showed me the chimpanzees and I liked them," says Freddie. The truth is, Freddie's wife was taking an art class from Jose and it was she who first brought the paintings to Freddie's attention. The paintings seemed to match the animal-print carpet Freddie had put down in the restaurant and so Jose was commissioned to fill the bar with monkeys. One special piece shows a white-suit-clad Freddie dancing hand-to-paw with a chimpanzee in a skirt. The Monkey Bar, where according to Linda, "People go to monkey around," is one of the most popular parts of Piero's. Here you might find singer Pia Zadora entertaining guests or Frank and Deano impersonators crooning to the audience in a scene reminiscent of an old Las Vegas lounge.

Sure, the food's beyond compare and sure, you're certainly treated well at Piero's, but there are other restaurants in Vegas that serve amazing food and there are other restaurants in Vegas that treat you well, so what is it that makes this place so different? That "it," whatever "it" may be, is what makes Piero's so special. When you walk in the door you may not be able to put your finger right on it, but it's there. Piero's has "it." Maybe what makes Piero's great is that it isn't trying to be great, it just is. Here you can walk in, have a one-of-a-kind meal, and get treated like you're part of the family. Linda hits it right on the nose when she says, "We're thankful for you." Evan, too, understands what that "it" is. "We take care of people the way they should be taken care of," he says. "People know we're going to go that extra mile. It's much more than being attentive, it's heartfelt. There's a lot of love in the place."

PINBALL HALL OF FAME

1610 E. TROPICANA AVE. • LAS VEGAS, NV 89119

(702) 597-2627 • PINBALLMUSEUM.ORG

He's a Pinball Wizard

*J*f you can't remember the last time you played a pinball machine, you're probably not alone. But if you can't remember the last time you played a pinball machine from the 1940s or 1950s, it's probably because you just haven't been to the Pinball Hall of Fame. Started as the brainchild of Michigan native Tim Arnold, the Pinball Hall of Fame, also called the Pinball Museum, has 206 games, 152 of which are pinball machines. The oldest was built in 1947 and the newest in 2009.

If you ask Arnold—whose title is the Director of Stuff and Things—why he started the pinball museum he'll tell you quite simply, "Me and several other guys really like pinball." The true story, however, goes much deeper. In the 1960s and '70s pinball machines were everywhere. They could be found in five-and-dimes, grocery stores, cafeterias, Laundromats, and even barbershops. Pinball machines from that era were based around themes like the Wild West, horse racing, baseball, travel, gambling, surfing, and even futuristic life in space. A quarter would get you three balls—called plays—and when you achieved certain predetermined levels, you got additional free plays. If you were good enough, you could play for hours on a single quarter. But the learning curve was high.

This didn't stop people like Arnold, who at the tender age of sixteen had already developed into a bit of a pinball wizard. While still in high school, he bought his first machine and set it up in his garage, charging the neighborhood kids ten cents a game to play. Seeing how popular the machine was with his friends, Arnold bought

more machines and placed them in Laundromats and grocery stores around town. By 1976, at only twenty years of age, he opened his first pinball arcade in Lansing, Michigan—later opening another in Ann Arbor. Not only did he run the arcades, he fixed all the machines himself. By 1990 Arnold was ready for "retirement," so he sold his arcades to his younger brother Ted and made the move to Las Vegas.

Through the years, Arnold had accumulated nearly one thousand pinball machines in his personal collection. This collection, which is one of the largest in the world, was started almost by accident. You see, when a new machine comes out, the local distributer will often give a credit to the arcade, taking away the old machine and scrapping it for parts. At the time he owned his arcades, the credit was fifty dollars. Arnold just couldn't stand to let these beautiful machines be scrapped for such a low price, so he kept them, and when he moved to Las Vegas, he took his machines with him.

Arnold's love for pinball machines had brought him a certain amount of wealth—not that he was super rich, but he didn't have to work and he wanted to give back to his community. In 1993 he started holding pinball parties, which he called Fun Nights, an essential part of which was raising money for local charities while people played the games they loved. The parties were so popular they inspired Arnold to form the Las Vegas Pinball Collector's Club (LVPCC), whose goal was to buy a building where the machines could be housed, not for display, but to be played. The club reached their goal and on January 13, 2006, the Pinball Hall of Fame opened its doors to the public.

Unlike other museums, the Pinball Hall of Fame has no entry fee. All you need is a roll of quarters and a bit of time. With older machines, one quarter will still get you three balls; however those three balls will cost you fifty cents with newer machines. If you're into flashy lights, loud noises, and digital displays, if you're looking for games decorated with pop-culture icons such as Superman, the Addams Family, James Bond, Lord of the Rings, Star Wars, and Star Trek, the games from the 1980s, '90s, and 2000s are for you. However, if you want a taste of the vintage, bypass these loud machines and head to the row featuring pinball machines from the '40s, '50s, '60s, and '70s.

Walking down these rows, it's easy to recall a time when players could be seen throwing a hip into the corner of a pinball machine at just the right moment to make the ball change course or activating the flippers when the ball is in the sweet spot to make it fly up and to the right of the field to get that much-desired bonus. These machines were much simpler than their present-day counterparts and the goal of every player was the same: hit as many discs, targets, and flashing devices as possible to get the highest score so that you could continue to hit as many discs, targets, and flashing devices as possible.

In this row you can play poker at the Big Casino, catch a magic show with Flipper, race cars with Stock Car, or enjoy America's pastime with Baseball. You can race horses with Foto Finish, kick a soccer ball with Kicker, go skydiving with Sky Jump, live out your fantasy with Rock Star, or find a beautiful alien in Space Walk. Or you can choose the 1966 Magic Baseball game, which features a twelve-inch doll of a male child in a felt gray baseball uniform, complete with hat. The player operates the doll, who holds a bat, which is used to hit balls for a home run. The game was once part of the Midway at Circus Circus when it opened in 1967. It was removed from the Midway in 1968 and placed into a warehouse, where it was stored until 2009 when Arnold bought the game and rebuilt it.

But if you're really looking for vintage, you have to find the games in the real wooden cabinets with the exposed wood trim. The ones with only two flippers and no score counters. You have to find the games pioneered by Gottlieb, Chicago Coins, and Bally's (which is now most famous for making slot machines). Games such as Lady Robin Hood, a 1948 post-war pinball machine that has the rather risqué image of a woman in cutoff shorts, strapless bra, and a feathered Peter Pan-style cap, holding a bow and arrow.

While the Pinball Hall of Fame is possibly the only place you can find so many machines in one place, the best part isn't the pinball machines at all. In fact, it isn't even the arcade games, the rare one-of-a-kind games, or that the place is open seven days a week. The best part of the Pinball Hall of Fame is the members of the LVPCC who donate their time to run the place and work on the machines. It's Tim Arnold, who doesn't collect a salary for his work. "It's hard to spend money when you're working all day," he says.

So you may ask what happens to all the quarters played into the machines. Who collects the revenue? The answer to that question is what makes the Pinball Hall of Fame special. What doesn't go toward maintenance and upkeep goes to Arnold's reason for opening the hall of fame in the first place: charity. Over the years the Pinball Hall of Fame has given millions of dollars to local charities. In fact, they average a half-million dollars in charitable donations every year. Which just goes to show you that pinball machines never went away. What left were the places where you could find them and play them. But now, once again, there's a place to play all the machines you once loved—a place where you cannot only relive your childhood, but also feel good about doing it.

PLANT WORLD NURSERY

5311 W. CHARLESTON BLVD. • LAS VEGAS, NV 89138

(702) 878-9485 • PLANTWORLDNURSERY.COM

A Nursery or a Menagerie

*A*s soon as you enter Plant World, you get the feeling this isn't your typical nursery. Sure, there are plants of all kinds—succulents, herbs, trees, and all manner of flowers—but there are also more than fifty exotic birds, five cats, three tortoises, several geckos, twenty red-tipped water turtles, koi fish, and at least one dog. Plant World was started in 1967 by Jerry Harrison, who once worked at Heinz Ketchup. Jerry originally opened the store on the corner of Charleston and Decatur, but moved it up the street when the larger property became available.

Jerry's son Jay—a master horticulturist—worked on his father's ten-acre property after graduating high school, starting as a loader and gate boy. In the summers, Jay interned at a Japanese growing center in Torrance, California, which explains why Plant World not only sells bonsai plants, but the tools needed to shape and prune them. Jay—who served on the board of directors for the Nevada State Board of Agriculture—stayed in the family business, working his way up the ladder, becoming a salesman, buyer, assistant manager, manager, and eventually the owner in 1989.

Over the years, Plant World has stayed in business by offering just about everything your gardening heart could desire. If you want to grow bamboo, they can help you do that. If you want to start a vegetable garden, they not only have the plants you need, they can also help you prepare the soil, teach you how to feed the plants once they've sprouted, and tell you the best time to harvest. If you want to plant a fruit tree, Plant World has nectarine, cherry, apricot, peach, apple, plum, pear, and pomegranate trees. Heck, they even have fig trees. At Plant World you can find planting soil—a necessity in the Nevada desert—as well as a wide assortment of colorful pots; all types of garden art; and, scattered around the nursery on posted signs, helpful gardening hints like, "Spray roses with insecticide in the evening to eliminate mites and aphids." If you want to grow orchids or fancy houseplants, Plant World has a four-thousand-square-foot greenhouse—the largest in Las Vegas—with just about everything you could ever want or need.

But maybe the best thing about Plant World has less to do with plants and more to do with atmosphere. "We have a percentage of people who just come here to relax and get a little peace of mind," says Jay. To understand just what he means, all you have to do is take a stroll around the grounds. Intermixed among the roses, orchids, and fruiting trees are green-nape Amazons, greater sulfur-crested cockatoos, yellow-nape Amazons, blue and gold macaws, Swainson's toucans, military macaws, and scarlet macaws—to name only a few—sitting in cages or out in the open on perches high above the ground. "We have just about every kind of parrot," says Jay, who used to breed exotic birds in his backyard. When he took over the property he brought his birds with him. "Then people just started giving them to us," Jay says, explaining how he ended up with more than fifty birds.

One of the most well-known birds on the property is Delilah, a fourteen-year-old white cockatoo who makes Plant World her home. "We do tours and offer educational programs," says Jay, and Delilah is often the star. In fact, children from schools all over Las Vegas come to Plant World to see the animals. After a tour of the property, the children are brought over to Delilah, who loves to put on a show. She dances, plays dead, and bobs her head to her own imaginary beat. She also says some words like "Hello" and "Bye."

The person leading the tour is most often Richard "Sully" Sullivan. "I enjoy the tours," says Sully, who, after retirement, moved to Las Vegas from Maryland with his wife. "I have a good time talking to the kids and showing them around." Sully loves the tours so much he even comes in on his day off if needed. Besides giving tours, Sully takes care of the birds, many of which have been born on the property. Sully's job is to make the birds feel comfortable, ensure they have food

and water, and to keep their cages clean. It's a job he takes very seriously. Sully loves the birds and you can tell. "They've all got a story," says Sully about the birds. "Some were bought, some were rescued, and some were born here." When the weather is good, Sully takes the birds out of their cages and places them on the many perches around the property. "We can't take them out when it's windy," explains Sully. "They'll get a chest cold."

It would seem the birds like visitors as much as visitors like birds. As you pass by they'll watch you and, in some cases, speak to you. They'll pose when you take their picture and some of them will even try to climb on you if you get too close, although that is not recommended because many of the birds will bite. That is why when visiting Plant World, it's best not to pet the birds, but you can take all the photos you want.

Of course, exotic birds are not the only draw to Plant World. Toward the back of the property are three African spurred tortoises, second in size only to the giant tortoises on the Aldabra and Galápagos Islands. The tortoises—Bertha, Princess, and Ziggy—live in an enclosure where they are fed a special blend of hay and such specialties as watermelon. "They love watermelon," says Sully. "They get it all over their faces." Kids love to touch the tortoises and just watch them move around. However, tortoises are not the only reptiles at Plant World. There is also a large collection of water turtles, which hang ten on a surfboard or sun themselves on rocks in a koi-filled pond, complete with a waterfall.

But what really makes Plant World special, what has allowed them to stay in business for nearly fifty years, is how they treat their customers. "We concentrate on quality and service," says Jay. In fact, Plant World doesn't just sell you a plant; they tell you how to grow it, where to plant it, and what plant works best in the sun or in the shade. However, if you only want to hang out, you're welcome to do just that. In fact, it's not uncommon to see people simply wandering around with their own pets, looking at the birds, turtles, tortoises, and, of course, the plants. Plant World isn't just a nursery. It's a community; a place to gather and decompress after a long, hard day. So even if you don't have a garden, or even if you don't own a plant, you're always welcome at Plant World—no green thumb required.

RETRO VEGAS

1131 S. MAIN ST. • LAS VEGAS, NV 89104

(702) 384-2700 • RETRO-VEGAS.COM

Selling Lost Vegas

Although casinos have been in Las Vegas in one form or another for more than a hundred years, the era most closely associated with Sin City is the 1950s and '60s, a time when crooners ruled both the charts and the showrooms on the Strip. A time when the mob took an active role in the operation of most casinos. And a time when nuclear bombs were exploded at a test site close enough to town that mushroom clouds could not only be seen on a regular basis, but appeared on many postcards as well.

This is the era celebrated by Retro Vegas, a store selling antiques, furnishings, accessories, and art. Walk into the pink building just one street west of the famous Las Vegas Strip and you'll be instantly transported back to a time when Las Vegas was still a small town, when gambling was contained to casinos, and Frank, Sammy, and Dean performed nightly in the famous Copa Room. As soon as you walk through the front door you're greeted by an eclectic mixture of the practical and impractical. Where else in Vegas are you able to find a set of four rare teak compass chairs designed by Erik Kirkegaard next to a seven-foot replica of Michelangelo's *David*?

But Retro Vegas is more than a simple antiques store. It is a place to find time-forgotten treasures. Retro Vegas is most likely the only place in town where you can purchase a marquee from the Forum Shops in Caesars Palace or a welcome mat from the bygone Desert Inn. It is certainly one of the few places in Vegas where you can buy an ashtray from the Thunderbird Casino, the Holiday Casino, or the Barbary Coast—all of which have long since had a date with the wrecking ball. And while you may still be able to go to the Tropicana or the Palace Station to get an ashtray, you won't be able to get one from those casinos that dates back to the 1950s or '60s. For that you'll have to go to Retro Vegas.

Retro Vegas was started only six years ago by Bill Johnson and Marc Comstock, partners in life and in business. "The original name of the store was going to be the Pack Rat, a play on the famous Rat Pack," says Bill who used to be the director of the National Atomic Testing Museum. "But when we went to register the name, it had already been taken, so we chose Retro Vegas." It's an era that Bill and Marc not only sell, they also live. Several years ago the two bought the house once owned by one of Las Vegas's most famous residents, Jackie Gaughan, once owner of the El Cortez Casino. Gaughan, Sam Boyd, and Lester "Benny" Binion were the major players in town long before the mob, Steve Wynn, or MGM came a-calling.

If you're lucky, or if you simply ask, Bill and Marc will show you the inside of the home they redecorated by pulling out the article written about it, and them, in a local publication, the *Las Vegas Weekly*. Their home is a more sophisticated reflection of their store—although there is much more orange in the home. "We're into orange," Marc says,

Vintage Spots

GYPSY CARAVAN: EST. 1990

True to its name, this unique antiques store has been located in many different places around Las Vegas. In its current location since 1999, it offers a wonderfully eclectic mixture of vintage and one-of-a-kind items. The owner, Veronika, has created an inviting not-to-be-missed space that celebrates antiques, art, music, and food all in a set of railroad cottages that date back to the 1920s. Where else in Las Vegas can you find a saddled, stuffed mountain goat or an actual caboose still on its tracks?

1306 S. Third St.; (702) 868-3302

AMBERJOY'S VINTAGE CLOSET: EST. 2014

Okay, admittedly the date on this one hardly makes it vintage, but Amberjoy's just proves you don't have to be old to be vintage. Here you can find retro clothing—some from the period and others that are Amberjoy originals. They also offer vintage hair and make-up classes, and once you're done being made up, you can get your pinup photo taken in their private studio.

1225 S. Main St.; (702) 825-2020;
amberjoysvintagecloset.com

clothed in an orange camouflage jacket. "We've always been interested in midcentury stuff," Bill adds. "Our house is decorated that way."

While Retro Vegas is a relative newcomer to Las Vegas, it has spawned a renaissance of the old on Main Street. "We were the first in the area," Bill explains. "Then other antique stores started moving in about two years ago." There are now more than fifteen stores selling antiques and art in an area that has been dubbed Antique Alley. Maps of the stores in the alley, which Bill and Marc produce but which are paid for by contributions from each business owner, are available at the counter.

But while other antiques stores have opened in the area, few match the charm of Retro Vegas. In the back corner of the building sits a pink 1960s-era kitchen that has been transported—in its entirety—from the past to the present. The kitchen comes complete with metal two-door cabinets, a double-bowl sink, a Frigidaire refrigerator, and a top and bottom oven set with a glass window, all in—you guessed it—pink. About the only thing that changes in the kitchen is the table set, which has the annoying habit of getting purchased. At times the set has taken many forms, from a square laminate four-chair model to its current rectangular eight-chair design. The mainly metal chairs have also sported many different colors on their plastic surfaces, from a plain yellow to the current flower-patterned aqua blue. Opening the cabinets reveals a collection of glasses and plates that perfectly match the era of the kitchen and look as if they had been there since the '60s.

Stroll around the store and you'll find avocado-green couches and plastic-wrapped chairs, along with sets of tables and benches from old diners. You will also find a six-foot bronze giraffe, an Egyptian mummy tomb, and a signed poster advertising the *Bal du Moulin Rouge*, a show that once ran at the Las Vegas Hilton and starred Suzanne Somers. "We go to estate sales every weekend," Bill says, explaining how he and Marc are able to amass such a collection.

Once the purchases are made, the partners do the necessary research to find out where the item originated. They're pretty good at finding things out, but sometimes they have to rely on their patrons to tell them. At one point the partners had a pair of old seahorses in the shop whose origin they were unable to verify. That is, until the creator of *Splash*, a once long-running show in Las Vegas, came into the store and asked, "How'd you get my seahorses?"

RICK'S RESTORATIONS

1112 S. COMMERCE ST. • LAS VEGAS, NV 89102

(702) 366-7030 • RICKSRESTORATIONS.COM

Restoring Memories for Over Thirty Years

*J*f you ask Rick Dale how he got into the restoration business he'll tell you, "I needed to pay my house payment." The truth is, Rick has been restoring things all his life. He rebuilt a bicycle when he was only nine years old, and by fifteen he had progressed from bicycles to motorcycles to cars. "I was always into building stuff," Rick explains. "I've been restoring stuff since I was a kid."

You only have to spend a little time with Rick to see his love for restoration come through. "I love paint," he says. "I love taking things apart and I love putting things back together." Rick's restoration roots grew from his parents' gas station. "I loved those old pumps," Rick says, recalling his days as a gas-station attendant. "I wore that little hat and uniform." he says. Although it's a little hard to picture a man in worn blue jeans and a shirt with the sleeves torn off and showing off tattooed arms, ever wearing a gas-station attendant's uniform.

Of course, there is an element of truth in Rick's comment about needing money to pay his bills. In the early '80s Rick's construction business wasn't doing so well and Rick was struggling to make ends meet. Then he remembered the Rose Bowl Flea Market in Pasadena, California. "At the time, restored Coke machines were becoming a big thing overseas," says Rick, who just happened to have a Coke machine. He put a little over a thousand dollars into the restoration, took it to the flea market, and easily sold it for three times what he had into it. "It was a cheap buy and an easy restoration," Rick said.

That Coke machine led Rick down a new road. He started buying all the machines he could get his hands on, restoring them, and then

delivering them all over the country. "I started running around the country to sell pieces and along the way I started picking," explains Rick. Which means he'd buy items, like Coke machines, from people he'd meet in his travels. "I'd buy stuff and fill my truck," stuff that he would then restore and start the whole process over again.

Rick did restorations for ten years, starting in 1983. In that time he built a strong, steady business with a base of returning clientele. "The people we did machines for always called us back," says Rick, who grew his business long before the days of the Internet and social media; a time when word of mouth meant more than comments on sites like Yelp or Facebook ever could. Rick took great pride in restoring an object to its original glory. He'd research the piece, learn about it, and then make sure it was restored back to its original.

In 1993 Rick's personal life took a turn and he got divorced. That same year he closed his shop, sold it, and bought a horse property with corrals. He turned the corrals into workspaces and began operating the business out of his home. Things were a little tight then. When Rick restored something he often placed that item on the street out in front of his house in hopes of selling it. He slowly built the business again until 2007 when he decided he was done; he was ready to wrap it up and find something new to do. And then he met Kelly—the woman who would steal his heart.

Kelly convinced Rick to keep doing the thing he loved. "You do the work, and I'll make the money," Kelly told him. Kelly, who specialized in marketing, helped Rick take the business to new heights. Things were going exceptionally well when Rick was approached by the producers of the television show *Pawn Stars* and asked if he wanted to pawn a gas tank he had listed in the paper. Rick wasn't interested in pawning a tank he could sell for much more money, but he was interested in something else. He offered to be an expert on the show—the one who tells the *Pawn Stars* guys what the item is and how much it's worth. He was brought on the show and soon had episodes revolving around restorations he did for Rick Harrison, owner of Gold and Silver Pawn, the shop portrayed in the show.

Before long Rick was offered his own show—*American Restoration*—and since then he, Kelly, and the entire family have been on a bit of a rollercoaster ride. The first thing Rick and Kelly discovered was filming a television show out of a house not designed to film a television show made running the business a little difficult. "The production crew would want us to stop fabricating because they were recording one of us talking and they didn't want the background noise," explains Rick. This made it very difficult to keep a delivery schedule for clientele. On top of that, as the show grew in popularity, people began showing up at Rick's house—unannounced. "They'd climb over the fence," Rick says.

It soon became apparent to Rick and Kelly that a shop was needed, one that allowed them to both film the show and run their business. That was when they moved to their current location on Commerce Street. Now they can run their business, film the television show, and still cater to their fans' needs. Rick's Restorations is open to the public. The outside of the building is designed to look like a small town. There is a bank, a diner, and a movie theater—all named after members of the family. Inside is a gift shop and all manner of items Rick and his crew have restored that are available for sale. You can find items like gas pumps, round gas-station lights, Coke coolers, jukeboxes, and antique radios.

Stepping into Rick's shop is like stepping back into history. "When you come here it's a history lesson," says Rick. It's history you can

Vintage Spot

GOLD AND SILVER PAWN SHOP: EST. 1988

While this downtown pawnshop has been in business for close to thirty years, they are probably best known for their History Channel television show *Pawn Stars*. If you're looking for old collectables, one-of-a-kind items, or just really cool stuff, this is the place to go.

713 S. Las Vegas Blvd.; (800) 826-0292; gspawn.com

see if you take one of the free tours of the facility, where you'll find such things as a restored dog-tag machine, a rare Royal Crown soda machine valued at around forty thousand dollars, and a collection of pedal cars—all of which are available for purchase. You'll also see the massive sign Rick used to propose to Kelly and the bicycle built for two they rode off into the sunset.

On the free tour you get to watch the craftsmen plying their trades and even get a sneak peek at some of the items that will be featured on future episodes of the show—such as an old arcade boxing machine. Tours are also available that take you behind the scenes, giving you a view of both the work areas and the "bone yard" where Rick keeps items you can purchase and have restored—like refrigerators, popcorn machines, old arcade games, candy machines, and kiddie cars that used to cost a quarter to ride.

While Rick's life has gotten more hectic since the show first aired, having your own show does have its benefits. The production crew tends to find new and interesting things for Rick to restore and he loves it. "People come in and they tell me the story of the piece they want restored," says Rick. "They tell me how much it meant to them and it really touches me." This is easy to see by the expression on Rick's face when he talks about the items he's restored. And while the show may bring with it a certain amount of pressure, getting to touch these items, hearing the stories, and seeing the looks on people's faces when the item is restored makes all the work Rick and his crew puts in completely worth it.

Another benefit of having a successful show, and your own business, is you can get your family involved and Rick's Restorations is certainly a family affair—one that has made Rick a very happy man. Rick's brother Ron is a picker and his wife Kelly does research and development—besides running her own real estate agency. Their son Tyler runs the shop and their other son Brettly is both a salesman and a picker. Their daughter Ally is both the office manager and in charge of merchandise.

While Rick may have gotten into the business because he needed the money, he has walked away with something much more valuable. "Having the gratitude is way more awesome than having the money," he says. "The people who know the show and watch us love us, and that makes me happy, happy, happy."

SIENA ITALIAN AUTHENTIC TRATTORIA AND DELI

9500 W. SAHARA AVE. • LAS VEGAS, NV 89117

(702) 360-3358 • SIENAITALIAN.COM

A Taste of Italy

Siena has been the place where locals and tourists alike have been getting a taste of Italy for over thirty years, and while you don't have to speak Italian to come here, it helps. That's because the deli is, and has been, run by authentic Italian-speaking Italians, and its clientele is made up largely of Italian-speaking Americans. In fact, you won't be in the deli for any time at all before you hear Italian being spoken by both the employees and the patrons. Rest assured, however, that non-Italian speakers are just as welcome.

Siena Italian Authentic Trattoria and Deli got its start as Siena Deli in 1978. At that time it was run by a Sicilian family and was on the corner of Tropicana and Eastern, where it sat in the back of a shopping center. It was a popular location, but by 2006 the area fell on hard times. "It was the worst time in the economy," says Chef Giancarlo Bomparola, who along with Antonio Accornero purchased Siena in 2006. "We saw the potential of the business, but we needed to move it to a different area." That took the partners across town to Sahara Avenue where they found an existing restaurant. They refurbished the place, added the deli, and opened an Italian bakery. They also started doing catering.

It's hard to get more authentic than Chef Giancarlo. Born in Calabria, Italy, he was raised in Milano—that's Milan to you non-Italians. His family operated restaurants and so Chef Giancarlo got his start in the restaurant business at a very young age. By the time he was seventeen he had a job in one of the largest pastry shops in all of

Italy. Sometime in the early '90s Chef Giancarlo made his way to the United States, landing in San Diego. He stayed there for a while before heading to France to learn French culinary techniques. He eventually made his way back to America and worked for a company opening restaurants. After a time Chef Giancarlo left the company to open two restaurants of his own in Sacramento, California. After operating those restaurants successfully for several years, he sold them and moved with his brother to Las Vegas to start a consulting business. There he met Antonio and when the Siena Deli became available, the partners took a chance on a bit of Vegas history.

Siena, if you're wondering, isn't a surname, but the name of a town in the Tuscan region of Italy. The small Italian town of about 53,000 people is often called Italy's loveliest medieval city. It is also known for its famous Palio di Siena, which is a bareback horse race run around the city's main piazza—the Piazza del Campo. That would be like running a horse race around the downtown area of any town. The barely two-minute race was once even featured in the 2008 James Bond movie *Quantum of Solace*.

If it's Italian, Siena Deli has it. They work hard to earn the title of Autentica Cucina Italiana or Authentic Italian Kitchen. If you're looking for an honest-to-goodness pasta, you know, the large shells or those tubes perfect for stuffing, the kind you can't find in your typical grocery store, you'll find it at Siena Deli. If you prefer your pasta fresh, and stuffed, don't worry, they've got that too. A favorite of many is their ravioli and if your experience with ravioli is limited to that which comes out of a can from a chef named Boyardee, you're in for a treat. Real ravioli, the kind you want to eat, is cheese sealed between two layers of thin, square pasta dough, which are squeezed around the edges to create a sort of pillow. Throw them into some salted boiling water and leave them in there just until they rise to the top, then cover them in your favorite sauce, and you're all set. You can also choose cannelloni, which are pasta cylinders, typically stuffed with beef. These you put in the oven, covered with some great-tasting pasta sauce and possibly some cheese and bake them until they're hot and ready to eat. *Perfetto!*

One of Siena Deli's specialties is their fresh olives. Everyone loves olives, especially Italians. At Siena you can find fresh olives in just about every size and color. They have large bright green or red cerignola olives, golden Sicilian olives, and purple Greek and Kalamata olives, as well as the traditional small black olives. Along with olives they have red peppers, marinated artichokes, marinated mushrooms, calamari, and baccala, which is dried and salted cod. And what would an Italian deli be without a selection of rich Italian meats. They have Genoa salami, prosciutto, rosemary ham, and mortadella—a staple of Bologna made from ground, heat-cured pork sausage mixed with small cubes of pork fat. Siena deli is also one of the few places where you can find spek or smoked pork. This thin-sliced meat is made from only the very best and leanest legs of pork and if you haven't tried it, you need to and right away.

If cheese is more you're thing, they've got all the best vowel-ending cheese you could ever want. There's ricotta, pecorino Romano, fontina, locatelli, provolone, mozzarella, provaletta, Parmigiano, and mozzarella di bufala, or buffalo mozzarella. The name, as you might guess, comes from the fact that the cheese is made from the milk of a water buffalo. The taste of this creamy, smooth cheese is beyond compare and it is one of the most difficult cheeses to make, but Siena Deli does it and they do it well.

Siena Deli has shelves and shelves stocked with all manner of Italian staples, all imported from Italy. "We import products that are

Vintage Spot

CARNEGIE DELICATESSEN: EST. 2005

This famous deli, located inside the Mirage, is the Las Vegas branch of the New York deli, which opened on Seventh Avenue in 1937. Here you can find all your standard deli favorites including what was voted the #1 Pastrami Sandwich in all of New York against twenty-two other delis.

3400 S. Las Vegas Blvd.; (702) 791-7310; carnegiedeli.com

very hard to find," says Chef Giancarlo. Here you can find Italian olive oil and balsamic vinegar, pickled peppers and veggies, as well as just about every variety of roasted peppers. If you're looking for pasta sauce, you'll find some, but you're more apt to find canned tomatoes—both roasted and non-roasted—instead. This is because Italians tend to make their own pasta sauce instead of relying on sauce from a jar or, heaven forbid, a can.

Of course, no deli would be complete without a selection of sandwiches and Siena is no exception. Here you can choose from a variety of cold sandwiches made from the best Italian meats. If you prefer a hot sandwich, you can choose from chicken, eggplant, or meatball Parmigiana; peppers and eggs, sausage and peppers, or chicken and roasted peppers. Being a bakery, Siena can satisfy your sweet tooth as well with assorted cakes and cookies. But you can also get authentic tiramisu—which means "pick me up" in Italian—made traditionally with both espresso and dark rum, and the staple of any Italian deli—a cannoli. If you want to know if you've come to a real Italian deli—like Siena—check to see if they fill their cannoli to order. If they do, stick around. Cannoli are filled to order so the shell won't become soft, and any authentic deli knows that.

You might wonder if moving a deli to the other side of town would affect your business. If you ask Chef Giancarlo, his answer would be no. "Much of the old clientele still comes back from different places around town. Especially during the holiday season," says Chef Giancarlo. "But we have also established a much broader clientele who didn't know us when we were on the other side of town." Siena now has much more to offer than it had when it was on the corner of Tropicana and Eastern. Not only is there a deli, but there's a trattoria as well. A trattoria is a small restaurant serving simple food. Actually, "simple" is probably not the best word to describe the tortino di riso, gnocchi al pesto, tagliolini ai frutti di mare, or the pollo marsala served at Siena's Trattoria. *Delicioso* is a much more appropriate word.

SPRING MOUNTAIN RANCH STATE PARK

6375 HWY. 159 • BLUE DIAMOND, NV 89004

(702) 875-4141 • PARKS.NV.GOV

An Oasis in the Desert

When you mention Las Vegas, most people think of spectacular casinos and amazing shows, all in an adult-oriented atmosphere. They think of slot machines, poker tables, cocktail waitresses, and showgirls. And they think of heat . . . bone-searing heat. But that is not all Las Vegas has to offer. Located just fifteen miles west of Las Vegas is an oasis in the desert that was once a fully functional ranch with a storied past going back well into the 1800s.

In 1829 merchant Antonio Armijo led a group of sixty men and one hundred mules on a trek from Santa Fe, New Mexico, to Los Angeles, California. Looking to establish a trade route, Armijo chose trails blazed by trappers, traders, and mountain men, such as Jedediah Smith. He also created his own trails, connecting those existing into one main trail that could be used over and over again. When he got to the Mojave Desert, just before Death Valley, Armijo turned south, following the intermittent streams all the way to California. Armijo eventually arrived at the San Gabriel mission with his group, for the most part, intact—minus a few mules that were used for meat. The trail Armijo pioneered became known as the Spanish Trail and eventually the Mormon Trail. The point where the trail turned south was the area that would eventually be home to the Spring Mountain Ranch.

The ranch got its start in 1860 when a one-room cabin and blacksmith shop was built on land adjacent to the Spanish Trail. The area had become a stop along the way and although the origins of the

cabin and shop are unknown, the structures were most likely built to help mend wagons and provide a respite for weary travelers. In 1876 James B. Wilson and George Anderson homesteaded 350 acres and named it the Sandstone Ranch, using the Flying 5 brand. The two men raised cattle, providing meat and fruit to miners in the area and, starting in 1905, to the newly established town of Las Vegas. In 1906, after James's death, his adopted sons Jim Jr. and George "Tweed" Wilson took over operation of the ranch, eventually leaving it in the hands of George's son Buster. When World War I broke out, the ranch was mortgaged for an ill-thought-out venture into creating wagons for the war. The venture failed when the war ended before the operation could get off the ground.

A year later a fruit orchard was planted on the property, which remained in hock until 1929 when the mortgage was paid off by Willard George, owner of Willard George Furs. George built a home on the ranch below the original one-room cabin, changed the name to K Bar 2, and kept Buster on as the ranch manager. George owned the ranch until 1948 when he sold it to radio entertainer Chester "Chet" Harris Lauck, half of the famous Lum and Abner comedy duo. While Lauck only owned the ranch for seven years, it was under his direction that the ranch developed into its present incarnation.

With Buster's help, Lauck built a ranch house on the property, using sandstone quarried from the area. He built the walls of his New England–style home fourteen inches thick, making them self-insulating. He covered a portion of the exterior walls with redwood board, leaving the sandstone bare in some areas. Inside Lauck used beams from a plant in Henderson that was closing to support the roof. He shipped in used bricks taken from Alviso Street in Santa Clara, California, to build the fireplace. He built a pool out back and an elaborate kitchen, complete with copper-fronted ovens, a chopping-block table, and a hutch. He installed pine shelves and brought in pewter and copper cookware.

Lauck kept the cattle operation up and running, but changed the name of the ranch to the Bar Nothing Ranch. He built a large stone entranceway on which he attached a bronze plaque that read, "Chester Lauck's Bar Nothing Ranch formerly Wilson Ranch since 1874." He also posted signs around the ranch offering a five-hundred-dollar reward for "information leading to the arrest and conviction of anyone stealing any of my cattle," signing it C. H. Lauck.

In 1955 the ranch changed hands again, when it was bought by Vera Krupp, a German-born actress who had recently returned to Las Vegas from Essen, West Germany. Vera was married to Alfred Krupp, whose family built arms for Hitler's war machine. Alfred was eventually convicted for crimes against humanity, serving three years of a twelve-year sentence. Vera, who had married Krupp in 1952, chose to live in Las Vegas over Germany. She was the only person, after Jim B. Wilson, who both lived on and ran the ranch.

Vera changed the name of the property to Spring Mountain Ranch and used the brand Diamond V. She raised prized Herefords and Brahma bulls and could often be seen riding her horse Sweetheart around the ranch. Vera ran Spring Mountain Ranch for twelve years. On April 10, 1959, three armed men forced their way into the ranch house and ripped Vera's 33.6-carat emerald-cut diamond right off her finger. While the diamond was recovered six weeks later, Vera was worried about being on the ranch without the ability to call for help if needed. She paid to become an official deputy sheriff and even had a badge made with her name on it. Vera sold the ranch in July of 1967, the same month her husband died. She passed away three months later. Her famous diamond was sold to actor Richard Burton in 1968 for $305,000. He gave it to his then wife Elizabeth Taylor who wore it until her death in 2011. That same year the diamond was again sold, this time to a Korean theme park and resort for $8.8 million.

In 1967 billionaire Howard Hughes bought the ranch. He kept the name, but changed the brand to Hughes Tool, which was a capital T over a capital H. Hughes, who never lived on the ranch, sold it in 1972 to Fletcher Jones and William Murphy for $1.5 million. The two men had plans of turning the ranch into a large equestrian and residential development. However, their plan was strongly opposed by residents of Las Vegas who wanted to leave the property as it was. When both the Nevada Open-Space Council and the Red Rock Advisory Committee joined forces with concerned residents, the deal eventually fell through. Unable to see their plans fulfilled, the two men sold the ranch to the Nevada Division of State Parks who bought it through the sale of bonds and with the help of federal lands and water conservation funds.

The ranch house and property are now in the very capable hands of the state of Nevada, which also purchased an additional 178 acres, bringing the total acreage of the ranch to 528. The house originally built by Willard George was remodeled as a guesthouse by Vera Krupp and now serves as the ranger station. The original one-room cabin and blacksmith shop have been preserved and are still located on the ranch. The orchard has long since died, except for two remaining pear trees, which still produce fruit. The place where the orchard once stood is now a picnic area open to the visitors of the park.

Many of the artifacts that once called the ranch home are still there today. The actual branding irons from both Chet Lauck and Howard Hughes are prominently displayed, as are the reward signs Lauck posted around the ranch, and the bronze plaque he had made. Many of the Wilson family belongings—Duchess pattern bread and butter plates, salt and pepper shakers, and pilot's glass—are in a display case in what was once the breezeway between the house and the barn. Several of Vera Krupp's belongings are also on display in one of the house's bathrooms, including the sheriff's badge she had made and towels embroidered with her Diamond V brand. Photos of all the people who lived at, owned, or influenced what would become Spring Mountain Ranch are also on display around the ranch house.

Vintage Spots

FLOYD LAMB STATE PARK: EST. 1964

While the 2,040-acre park was bought by the city in 1964, the park, which is located in Tule Springs, has roots back to prehistoric times. Fossil remains of early mammoths, bison, horses, and camels have been found there. Tule Springs is a series of small lakes that served as a water source for the Paiute Indians who hunted, fished, and planted crops in the area. Before the city of Las Vegas bought the property, it was a working cattle ranch.

9200 Tule Springs Rd.; (702) 229-8100; lasvegasnevada.gov

OLD LAS VEGAS MORMON FORT: EST. 1855

The fort, which is now part of the Nevada State Parks system, was built by William Bringhurst and a group of men, sent by Brigham Young to establish an outpost and post office in the valley. The fort had 14-foot-high walls that were 150 feet long on each side, with bastions positioned on the northwest and southeast corners. Bringhurst and his group eventually left the area when they discovered they couldn't grow crops and the lead they thought they had discovered turned out to be unsuitable for smelting—it was later discovered that the "lead" was actually silver.

500 E. Washington Ave.; (702) 486-3511; parks.nv.gov

BONNIE SPRINGS: EST. 1952

The Wild Wild West is alive and well just a few miles outside of Las Vegas in a place called Bonnie Springs. Bonnie Levinson, the "Bonnie" of Bonnie Springs, was a dancer and ice skater in the 1950s. In 1952 she bought 115 acres of land near Red Rock Canyon along the Spanish Trail. She turned the area into an authentic Old West town and petting zoo.

16395 Bonnie Springs Rd.; (702) 875-4191; bonniesprings.com

If you're looking for a break from casinos, gambling, and the bustling crowds on the Las Vegas Strip, Spring Mountain Ranch is the place for you. Being 1,800 feet higher than Las Vegas, the ranch is routinely ten to fifteen degrees cooler than temperatures on the Strip. In the summer, the ranch is home to the Super Summer Theater, which hosts plays and musicals under the night stars. Many living history programs—costumed role playing, demonstrations, and reenactments of historic events—are also presented at the ranch, which can be rented out for weddings. Besides its history, possibly one of the best features of the ranch is Penelope the cow. A former 4-H project, Penelope was donated to the ranch several years ago. She's very gentle and loves to be petted when she sticks her head outside the white fence. If you do come to Spring Mountain Ranch, be sure to look her up, and you may want to bring apple slices . . . and maybe carrots.

TIFFANY'S CAFE

1700 S. LAS VEGAS BLVD. • LAS VEGAS, NV 89104

(702) 444-4459 • TIFFANYSCAFELV.COM

Breakfast at Tiffany's . . . Cafe

*I*t's almost impossible to find the type of dining counter that was once common to such five-and-dimes as Woolworth's, Sines, Kresge's, or Newberry's. Impossible, that is, unless you travel to Tiffany's Cafe inside the White Cross Market in downtown Las Vegas. There you'll find a long, narrow diner with a long, narrow linoleum counter, complete with padded seat-style stools and a brass railing running along the bottom of the counter, just off the floor, on which to rest your feet. Once you take your seat, the plastic-encased menu is waiting in a black, metal menu holder screwed into the counter on the far side.

Resting near each menu are salt and pepper in glass shakers with metal caps. To the left of these staples is sugar. Not packets of Sweet 'n Low, Equal, Splenda, Sweet Thing, or even Sugar in the Raw. At Tiffany's, you won't find sugar in packets at all. Instead, what you get is actual white sugar in a large, ribbed-glass container with a metal cap that has a little lid that pivots open when the container is tilted sideways and closes when the container is returned to upright. Small white plastic packets of cream with paper lids that must be torn off sit in a bowl between the sugar and the salt and pepper. You almost expect the butter to be served on a wax-paper pad; it isn't. The feel of the cafe all harkens to a simpler time when twenty-four-hour diners were commonplace, when food cooked from scratch was affordable, a fountain drink cost you ten cents, and the waitresses knew your name.

In 1960 when it first opened its doors, the building that now houses White Cross Market was known as White Cross Drugs, a pharmacy that served locals, tourists, and stars such as Elvis, Dean Martin, and Frank Sinatra. White Cross Drugs was convenient for three main reasons: it was a neighborhood pharmacy, it was the only pharmacy on the Strip, and it was the first pharmacy in Las Vegas to stay open twenty-four hours a day. Nestled inside the drug store was Tiffany's Cafe, named after the Tiffany-style, stained-glass light fixtures that hung high above the counter. Also open twenty-four hours, Tiffany's became popular with hosts, dealers, showgirls, and all manner of casino employees who frequented the cafe in search of a well-earned meal. The restaurant served great food at reasonable prices and soon became known not only to locals, but also to tourists and the stars who shined nightly on the Las Vegas Strip.

Not much has changed at Tiffany's since then. Except, of course, for its owner. In the late 1970s Teddy Pappas came to America from Greece at the tender age of twenty-four. Although he originally landed in New York, Teddy eventually made his way to Las Vegas where he took a job cooking at Tiffany's. Twenty-one years later he bought the place and has owned it for the past twelve years. When asked why people keep coming back, Teddy has a quick, simple answer: "It's the quality of our food. Quality is our recipe." He points to the sign on the wall proclaiming just that. "Nothing is frozen," Teddy explains. "We make the soup from scratch. We make the gravy from scratch. We make everything from scratch." He pulls out the top round he was about to bread for chicken-fried steaks. "There are no fillers," he explains, holding up the meat, "just steak. Where are you going to find that anymore?"

In additional to being made from scratch, the food is cooked in front of the customer. In fact, nothing is hidden at this cafe. Working just on the other side of the counter is exactly one cook and one server. The grill, broiler, and deep fryer are all open in front of the counter. And although the cook plies his trade with his back toward the counter, he frequently turns and engages in conversation with those eating or waiting for their food. On display in front of the customers, in full view, is just about everything Tiffany's needs to operate. Metal shelves are stacked high with easily accessible plates, cups, glasses, and to-go boxes. Coffee is brewed one pot at a time and decaf is not an option. If asked for decaf the server will simply say, "Our coffee is not strong." There is a small soda fountain and a cash

register that was probably manufactured in the late '70s or early '80s.

Above customers' heads, attached high on the wall, are two large plastic menus showing options for breakfast, lunch, and dinner. The menu is the kind where black letters are pressed into horizontal grooves on a white background to create words. Prices are made up of red numbers that are pressed into the same grooves just to the right of the menu items.

The food isn't fancy, but it is nonetheless good. A half-pound cheeseburger deluxe will run you $7.45 and will come with fries, onion slices, a crisp piece of lettuce, one tomato, and four pickles. Ketchup comes in a red picnic-style dispenser, while mustard is kept in its original container. Checks are still written on paper by hand. Used plates, cups, and utensils are collected by the server and placed into bins, hidden from view, on the backside of the counter.

Tiffany's is, as one might expect, most known for its breakfast. Three large eggs any style, home fries made from scratch, and toast will run you $4.95, while a three-egg steak omelet—the most expensive omelet on the breakfast menu—complete with mushrooms, onions, and peppers will set you back $8.95. Hand-breaded chicken-fried steak and three eggs any style, with homemade gravy and home fries, costs a whopping $8.50.

While it may be the food that beckons locals and tourists from all over the world, it is the service that keeps them coming back. "My regular customers know me," says Teddy. "If there is any problem with the customer I fix it. If they don't eat, I don't eat." Teddy, who has been in the restaurant business for more than fifty-three years, isn't going anywhere fast. "The customers keep me here," Teddy says, smiling. In 2012 White Cross Drugs was forced to close when their supplier unexpectedly cut them off from ordering drugs. The closing didn't faze Teddy. "You gotta give and take," he says. "That's life." So when White Cross Drugs closed and the new owner opened White Cross Market, Teddy signed a ten-year lease. This means that at least for the next decade you won't have to travel to New York to eat breakfast at Tiffany's.

TROP AQUARIUM

3125 E. TROPICANA AVE. • LAS VEGAS, NV 89121

(702) 458-2981 • TROPAQUARIUMLASVEGAS.COM

Aquatic Pets in the Desert

So many businesses come and go in Las Vegas that it can be hard to keep track of them all. Restaurants, retail stores, even casinos all have a shelf life in a city that always has one eye on the future. But there are some businesses that have managed to stay under the radar and not just hang on, but thrive. Trop Aquarium is one of those businesses. While the aquatic pet store, which services all your aquarium needs, has been around since 1978, its roots go back much farther. In 1960 aquarium hobbyist Harry Tetzlaff began breeding fancy guppies in his California home. Harry's hobby quickly grew from one tank to many and before too long, he realized it was time to open a store.

Keeping fish in bowls dates back to the early 1300s in China. However, it wasn't until the 1800s that such things as goldfish, eelgrass, and snails began to be contained in tanks, creating the first real "aquarium." In the early 1900s a pump was invented that could circulate the air inside the tank, creating a better environment. Later in the century when electricity became readily available, keeping fish in a home aquarium became popular. With the advent of silicone sealant, aquarium styles changed. Metal was left behind and all-glass aquariums became the norm. By the 1960s and '70s home aquariums were commonplace. Once Plexiglas came into the picture, aquariums could be molded into all manner of shapes and sizes.

Harry and his wife Belle opened their first aquatic pet store in 1968 in San Jose, California, at the height of the fish craze. Harry had become well known through his guppy breeding and had already established a clientele. The store allowed him not only to expand his breeding, but also to move into the sale of other type of fish and fish-tank supplies. The store proved so popular that two years later Harry and Belle had opened another store in San Jose. By 1974 the couple was ready for a change so they sold their stores and headed to Las Vegas. Four years later, in 1978, they decided to see if fish were as popular in a desert environment as they were in sunny California, so they opened Trop Aquarium in an outdoor shopping plaza on Tropicana Avenue. Within a very short time, they enjoyed the same success they had experienced in San Jose. That's when Dan Riggs and his wife Lisa—the daughter of Harry and Belle—entered the picture.

Dan had been working in nearby Arizona as both a dental hygienist and a drywall installer, and while he always did his best, he certainly didn't feel he'd found his calling. On one of his and Lisa's trips to Las Vegas to visit Lisa's parents, Dan took a second look at his in-laws' store and thought it might just be time for a career change. So he and Lisa packed up their belongings and, like Lisa's parents before her, moved to Las Vegas. While Lisa was excited, Dan was a bit apprehensive. "I didn't know anything about fish," he admits. "But my wife knew everything," he says with a smile. "Now I know a lot."

Dan is right—Lisa does indeed know a lot about fish and the environment in which they live. The Boulder City High School graduate learned much about aquatic pets under the tutelage of her parents. In fact, she became so knowledgeable that noted aquarium expert and author George Blasiola ranked Lisa the number one fish doctor in the country. This means Lisa doesn't just sell you fish when you come to Trop Aquarium; she helps you choose the right fish for the environment you are creating, tells you how to keep the fish happy and healthy, and can even diagnose your problems—but only the ones related to the aquarium.

No matter what your fish needs, they can be found at Trop Aquarium. Here you can get stones, plants, food, nets, lights, tanks, pumps, tubes, and all manner of interior tank decorations. If you want a castle in your tank, they have it. If you want a skull, sunken plane, or tiki hut for your fish to swim in and out of, you can find it here. If you want to set up a pirate ship with a full skeleton crew, they've got you covered. At Trop Aquarium you can get everything you need to set up either a fresh or saltwater tank. If you want, Trop Aquarium can even help you set up a reef tank, which is a tank that contains live corals as well as other marine invertebrates, and, of course, fish. "Reef tanks are becoming the big thing," says Dan.

The biggest seller at Trop Aquarium is, as you might expect, fish. "We sell around fifteen thousand fish a week," says Dan, "Mostly freshwater, because saltwater fish are more expensive." In fact, that is what you first see when you enter the doors of Trop Aquarium—rows and rows of fish in all shapes, sizes, colors, and varieties. They have koi fish, black gorilla umbis, giraffe cats, bala sharks, blood red parrots, African reeds, black ghosts, blueberry tetras, and tank-cleaning plecostomus to name but a very few. They even have lionfish. If your fish needs a companion, how about a fiddler crab or a turtle?

Just when the store was in the middle of its second decade, it almost had an unceremonious end. In 1991 an electrical fire swept through the shopping center, burning the store almost to the ground. "Everything was unrecognizable," says Dan. "When one of the firemen came out he asked me what kind of store it was. He couldn't tell." It was a total loss—well, almost. When the smoke cleared—literally—there was a single survivor, a red-eared slider turtle, which was renamed Smokey. When a business suffers such a loss, it's not

Vintage Spot

JOHNNY TOCCO'S BOXING GYM: EST. 1953

Johhny Tocco's Boxing Gym is a throwback to another era, one where boxers trained in a gritty gym complete with a ring, speed bags, heavy bags, jump ropes, and little else. Johnny was a trainer of champions, and the likes of Larry Holmes, Sonny Liston, Mike Tyson, and "Marvelous" Marvin Hagler have all trained in the gym under his watchful eye. While Johnny has retired, he's left his gym in the hands of a prominent boxing family who have honored Johnny's tried and true boxing traditions.

9 W. Charleston Blvd.; (702) 367-8269; jtboxing.com

uncommon for the owners just to let it go, but that wasn't the fate of Trop Aquarium. Instead of giving up, Dan and Lisa picked out a larger location in the same shopping plaza. They bought more supplies, stocked the store with fish, and reopened, because that's what their customers wanted. "We have an incredible clientele. They carried us. I have customers who still drive all the way from Summerlin," says Dan, referring to people who come from the other side of the valley just to get their fish at Trop Aquarium.

While the popularity of aquariums has waned in recent years, they're making a comeback with shows such as Animal Planet's *Tanked*. People watch those elaborate tanks being built on television and it renews their love for aquariums. Dan is a fan of *Tanked*. "*Tanked* has helped my business," he says. "They've done nothing but help the industry as a whole."

It's not often that you see a business last two generations, but Trop Aquarium is going on its third now that Dan and Lisa's daughter Nicole is working at the store. "Vegas has been good to us," says Dan. And if you ask him how he's managed to stay in business for so long, he'll tell you, "We don't cheat people. We try to treat them right." That's a recipe for success, no matter what business you're in.

VILLAGE MEAT AND WINE

5025 S. EASTERN AVE. • LAS VEGAS, NV 89119

(702) 736-7575 • VILLAGEMEATANDWINE.COM

Not Just Another Meat Market

*I*f you want beef, chicken, turkey, or pork, all you have to do is walk into any grocery store and you'll find just what you need. But what if you have a hankerin' for elk, wild boar, ostrich, or kangaroo? You won't find those meats in your typical grocery store. No, siree. For these more "exotic" selections, you'll have to go to a gourmet butcher shop, and in Vegas that means a trip to Village Meat and Wine. Located in an unassuming outdoor shopping mall, Village Meat and Wine has been fulfilling Las Vegans' more unique palates since 1977 when it was opened by Glenn and Emily Hare—a fitting name for the owners of a butcher shop that has rabbit as an offering.

At Village Meat and Wine you can find alligator ribs, elk ribs, and wild boar baby-back ribs, giving new meaning to the old jingle, "I want my baby back, baby back, baby back." If buffalo is your thing, you can get it ground, as tri-tip, or in a brisket. If you want lamb shanks, they've got it. Venison tenderloin? You bet. Cornish game hens, quail, duck breast, pheasant, or ostrich steaks? They have all those too. And if you want something a bit more exotic—like frog legs, camel, or alligator tail—Village Meat and Wine is the place to go.

Of course, if you want good old-fashioned beef, you can get that too because Village Meat and Wine is one of the few places in the valley where you can find natural, all-organic, hormone-free USDA prime beef. "The Kobe beef is our number one seller," says Tim Jenson who, sixteen years ago, along with his wife Chemaine, bought the property from its original owners. Tim likes to point out that he gets his Kobe from America and Australia, not Japan, and is more than happy to

show off the marbling inside the beef. "The fat is actually one of the healthiest of fats," he explains, adding that Kobe beef should always be cooked with the fat in place and then trimmed off before the meat is served. "The marbling is the butter," he says. "It's what gives the meat its flavor."

Although gourmet meat is their specialty, don't let the title of "gourmet" fool you. This isn't a stuffy, overpriced meat market catering only to the upper crust of Las Vegas society. While you may find a politician, judge, or personal chef in line beside you, you're just as likely to see a senior citizen or a family with children. "That's what makes this job fun," says Tim. "You never know who you're going to talk to." Village Meat and Wine is truly an old-fashioned neighborhood butcher shop. "We know most of our customers by name," says Chemaine. When you come in, they call you by that name, ask you how you are, and inquire about your family. "We're old school," says Chemaine. "Old Vegas was like this. Everybody treated you like family." It's a sentiment supported wholeheartedly by Tim. "We hang out with our customers," he adds. "We play golf with them and even go to dinner." Now that's making you feel at home.

Just as you'd expect a real butcher to do, Tim cuts your meat right in front of you. If you want ribs, he'll cut them. If you want steaks he'll cut them too. Of course you'll have to choose the thickness you want. This is done with blocks that show the actual size of the cut. If you want steaks cut to, say, one and a quarter inch, you'll get just that, steaks cut to an actual inch and a quarter—which, by the way, is much thicker than you'd expect. Besides feeling at home, you'll find the quality of the meats is beyond compare. Of course, you have to know how to cook the meat properly. But if you do, if you take the time to cook your Kobe steak the way it's meant to be cooked, you're in for a treat, the likes of which can only be found at a top-dollar gourmet restaurant. Fear not, though—if you're not sure how to spice your meat, you can purchase Tim's specialty rub. Much like the Colonel's, Tim's rub is made with a secret blend of herbs and spices that when added to your steak brings out just the right flavor to send your taste buds into orbit.

Originally, the assortment of wild game was much smaller than what is currently offered. However, as this type of meat became more popular, Tim and Chemaine increased the amount and types of wild game they kept on hand. "There's a lot of request for it in Las Vegas," says Chemaine, noting that it is especially popular with pet owners who grow increasingly dissatisfied with the quality of the pet food available. Many of these pet owners buy the wild game to make their own pet food. Of course, wild game isn't just for pets. "We like it," says Tim. "It's healthier for you."

Besides their high-quality meats, Village Meat and Wine has, well, wine. "People come in for a steak and buy a little wine," says Tim. It's not the $12.95 bottles you'd find in your typical grocery store, but the good stuff, the type you'd find in any gourmet restaurant, just not at gourmet prices. As Tim and Chemaine take their butcher shop into the future, they still keep a foot firmly planted in the past. And this doesn't just apply to their friends, family, and customers. It also applies to Village Meat and Wine's original owners, Glenn and Emily Hare, who every Thanksgiving are given a turkey and a bottle of wine by Tim and Chemaine. "They'll get that for life," promises Tim. It's his way of honoring the past.

WEST WIND
LAS VEGAS 6 DRIVE-IN

4150 W. CAREY AVE. • NORTH LAS VEGAS, NV 89032

(702) 646-3565 • WESTWINDDI.COM

The Best Kind of Stars

There is just something magical about a drive-in. For some reason, it's an entirely different experience seeing a movie in your car under the open sky, in the dark of night, with the twinkling stars shining down. When I was a kid, my folks would pack me and my pajama-clad siblings into the family station wagon and take us to the drive-in. I remember swinging on the swings right under the large, white screen, waiting for the movie to start. There was typically a cartoon or two, followed by a soda, candy box, popcorn, and some unidentifiable container of goodies—which I suspect was supposed to be a chocolate bar—dancing in a straight line singing, "Let's all go to the lobby. Let's all go to the lobby. Let's all go to the lobby to get ourselves a treat." It was your cue not only to buy refreshments from the concession stand, but that the movie was about to start.

When I was old enough to date, the drive-in was a favorite spot. We'd bring blankets and instead of sitting in the car, my date and I would sit on the hood. Watching a movie, no matter what movie, outside is a one-of-a-kind experience—one that stays with you long after the movie has faded from your memory. And I'm not the only one that feels that way. The 1950s and '60s were the heyday of the drive-in. According to the United Drive-In Theater Owner's Association, close to four thousand drive-ins opened in the US in 1958. By 2010 that number had dropped to a mere 370. It's understandable; the movie experience at a drive-in is dependent upon many factors. It has to be dark, meaning drive-ins sit empty during the day. It can't be raining, it shouldn't be windy, and it has to be relatively warm outside because you can't keep your car running. Indoor theaters suffer from none of those limitations. As with many things in the modern life, drive-ins stopped being popular a long time ago. That is, except in Las Vegas.

Just to the south of the North Las Vegas Airport, next to the Fiesta Rancho and Texas Station casinos, is a remnant from Las Vegas's past, the West Wind Las Vegas 6 Drive-in Theatre. The 950-car drive-in, which originally opened in 1965, was first known as the Las Vegas 6 Drive-in. When the drive-in opened almost fifty years ago, it had one large, white screen. Over the years, five more screens were added, bringing its current total to six. Although its original screen was destroyed in a storm in 1998, the drive-in has stayed in business since its opening.

Las Vegas has had a rich drive-in history. At one time there were six operating drive-ins scattered throughout the valley. The oldest was the Stardust Drive-in. Originally known as the Motor-Vu Drive-in, it was built in 1948 and was located on Stardust Lane behind the Stardust Casino. The 525-car, single-screen theater was eventually torn down to make room for Budget Suites. Another popular drive-in, the eight-hundred-car Skyway Drive-in, was located on Boulder Highway.

In 1981 it was closed and eventually torn down to make way for the Boulder Station Casino, which now sits where the drive-in used to be. The Sunset Drive-in, located on West Cheyenne, was closed in 1983. The Desert 5 Drive-in on South Lamb was eventually replaced by the Desert 16 indoor theater—which has also since been demolished. The largest drive-in in Las Vegas was most likely the twelve-hundred-car, single-screen Nevada Drive-in, which was located on Salt Lake Highway in North Las Vegas. A tattoo parlor now sits on the land where the theater used to be.

"The drive-in is more popular than you might think," says Tony Maniscalco, vice president of marketing for Syufy Enterprises, which bought the Las Vegas 6 Drive-in in 2006 and added West Wind to the name. It is easy to see why the drive-in is so popular. For seven dollars a person—five dollars on Tuesdays—you get to see two movies—what used to be called a "double feature." If you take your kids and they're between the ages of five and eleven, it'll cost you a buck a kid. Anyone under five is free.

After you pay for your chosen movie, you're directed to the proper screen and told where to park. Coming sooner gets you closer to the screen and coming later gets you farther away. However, as they say, there isn't a bad seat in the house. In the old days, once you chose your spot, you rolled down your window and lifted a speaker off a pole next to your car. The speaker, which was wired to the pole, was then hung on the car's window, which was typically rolled back up. How the movie sounded depended entirely on how well your chosen speaker worked. At the West Wind Drive-in the speakers are gone, and so are the poles. Now the quality of the sound depends on the quality of your car's sound system. Instead of listening to the movie through an often poorly wired speaker, you tune into the appropriate radio station and the movie plays in your car, through your car's very own speakers. The sound is much better and you don't have to worry about driving away with the speaker still attached to your window.

Sitting in your car with six screens playing six different movies can at first be a tad distracting. However, once you get into your movie, you tend to forget the other ones are even there. That is, of course, assuming the movie you're watching is good enough to keep your attention. All the movies are projected out of one booth and when you're close to the booth, you can see the streams of light, shooting in all directions, coming from the projection windows. When there are six screens, you pay at the ticket booth for one screen. That means you get to see both the movies playing on that screen and that screen only. There's no sneaking over to see the movies on another screen. That would be like going into a different movie after you've seen the one you paid for in an indoor theater. Although there are no walls at a drive-in, boundaries still exist.

Just as with drive-ins of old, the West Wind Drive-in has a concession stand, which is adorned with soon-to-be-released movie posters. Inside you can get snacks such as chocolate bars, cotton candy, and, of course, popcorn. You can also get nachos, hot dogs, hamburgers, cheeseburgers, pretzels, and soda. There is even a children's play area, only instead of being at the front of the screen, it is next to the concession stand.

When Syufy bought the drive-in, they not only changed the name, they updated the drive-in to digital projection. This makes the movies both clearer and easier to see, even when there are lights in the area. What they didn't change was the original neon sign. "When we bought the place we didn't know if the sign would work," say Tony, "but we turned it on and it lit right up." The sign, like the drive-in, is a throwback to the days when neon signs were a Las Vegas staple. The movie titles, which are displayed at the bottom of the sign, still have to be set with giant, black letters.

With the average cost of a movie in an indoor theater creeping around the eleven-dollar mark, it's hard to beat seven dollars for two movies, especially when a family of five can see those two movies for only seventeen dollars. Plus, when's the last time you went to an indoor movie theater in your pajamas?

Once a Dice Girl, Always a Dice Girl

J came here in December of 1948 to spend two weeks dancing and I never left," Nancy Williams Baker explains when asked what brought her from California to Las Vegas. She was eighteen years old and had a two-week contract with the El Rancho Vegas for seventy-five dollars a week. In 1948 the El Rancho Vegas was in full swing with more than one hundred rooms. It was located on what would later become known as the Strip, well out of town, and was the first resort-style hotel in Las Vegas.

As legend has it, businessman Tom Hull was traveling from California to Las Vegas in 1940 when he got a flat tire. While waiting for assistance, Hull couldn't help but notice the number of cars that were traveling down Highway 91 toward Las Vegas. The reason for Hull's visit was to meet with James Cashman, a car dealer and member of the Chamber of Commerce, and Robert Griffith, a prominent land developer. Hull owned a successful chain of resorts in California called El Rancho and the pair was hoping to entice him to expand the chain to Las Vegas. With his vehicle immobile, Hull had little to do but watch all the out-of-state license plates fly by. By the time he met with Cashman and Hull, he was primed and ready for their proposal and on April 3, 1941, Hull opened the El Rancho Vegas.

While casinos were becoming popular in Las Vegas, the desert town was still in the middle of nowhere. To get people to drive in from California—or anywhere else for that matter—many casinos started bringing in all manner of entertainment. They set up stages and opened showrooms. They brought in well-known singers, crooners,

dancers, and comedians. They also hired women as dancers to be on stage with the entertainers. These women—usually called "girls"—became a type of mascot for each casino. Sands had their Copa Girls and the El Rancho had their Dice Girls. Nancy was a Dice Girl.

In those days casinos were nowhere near as large as their present day incarnations. Showrooms were small and the stages inside the rooms were even smaller. "There were eight girls," Nancy says. "If you had nine girls, one would fall off the edge of the stage." Being only five feet, four inches tall, Nancy was always placed at the end of the line, a position that made her dance precariously close to the edge of the stage. Not only were the stages small, the dressing rooms were just as tiny. Typically there was only one dressing room and every-one—dancers and stars alike—used it.

One of the duties of a Dice Girl was to sit in the casino after the show and "dress up the joint," as the bosses used to say. Their duties also included showing up at events hosted or sponsored by the casino. During Las Vegas's Helldorado Days, Nancy and the other Dice Girls were "arrested," their bail going to charity. When a fire destroyed the El Rancho Vegas in 1960, Nancy went on to dance for the Thunderbird, the New Frontier, and eventually the Flamingo. However, a change was already taking place on the showroom stage.

During the time Nancy was dancing, a new type of "girl" began to take center stage. This showgirl was tall, slender, and mostly legs. "They started looking for tall girls," Nancy says. "Not short dancers like me."

In 1951 Nancy opened a dance studio. She was still dancing at night and was now teaching during the day. To show off the talents of her students, Nancy began holding recitals. She had plenty of students who had an abundance of talent. What she didn't have were outfits for her dancers. Nancy's mother was a costumer and under her tutelage Nancy had learned how to make costumes. So instead of purchasing the dancers' outfits for the recitals, Nancy began to make her own. She was so good at it that in 1954 she closed the dance studio and began concentrating entirely on costumes. At the time, her store was located across from the District Courthouse—the building that now houses the National Museum of Organized Crime and Law Enforcement, commonly called the Mob Museum. In 1975 she moved the business to its current location on Third Street and took up residency in the three-bedroom apartment above the store.

Over the years Nancy has made hundreds of thousands of costumes, so many that the second floor of her studio is filled with all manner of dresses, capes, hats, belts, shoes, and accessories. All hanging on racks. All waiting patiently to come back to life. Here you can

Vintage Spot
RaLPH JONES DISPLay: EST. 1965

Family owned and operated for more than four decades, Ralph Jones Display is for people who take their Christmas seriously. By specializing in the season of jolly 'ol Saint Nick, the retail store has become the go-to place to find all your jingle belly needs—no matter what time of year—and is a "secret source" for dedicated decorators both professional and amateur.

**2576 E. Charleston Blvd.; (702) 382-4398;
www.ralphjones.com**

choose from over one hundred Santa suits—both male and female—or, if you prefer, you can dress as a sexy skunk. If you're looking for the right costume for a themed wedding, Williams is your place, no matter what your wedding needs. If you want, the Williams Costume Company can dress you both as Elvis for a real Vegas-style wedding, or perhaps you'd prefer being married as Antony and Cleopatra or maybe as a famous crooner, like Dean Martin or Frank Sinatra, and a classic Vegas showgirl. No matter what your preference, Williams has your costume.

"We do good costumes," Nancy says, smiling. So good that Williams has become the go-to place for many of the performers and the casinos on the Strip. The great Liberace used to go shopping with Nancy and he bought all of his rhinestones from her. When Caesars Palace opened its doors to the public, Nancy made all the Roman-themed costumes worn by their greeters and hosts, many of which have been returned to her and are now available as rentals. However, if you don't like Roman costumes, you can wear one of Williams's specialties: a beautifully handcrafted Egyptian costume. "I love making Egyptian costumes," she says.

As more and more people began making their own costumes, Nancy saw an opportunity to expand her business. While holidays like Halloween and Christmas kept costume sales thriving, Williams began specializing in the materials people needed to build their own masterpieces. "I got into the sales stuff," she explains, "because people started asking for supplies." If you need rhinestones, Williams has them. If you need beads, Williams has them too. And if you need beards, feathers, fringe, trim, masks, hats, or theatrical make-up, Williams is your place. At eighty-four Nancy has no plans of going anywhere. "I'm gonna keep at it," she says. "Why go sit on a rock someplace? I get to meet new people and it's never dull."

YOUNG ELECTRIC SIGN COMPANY

5119 CAMERON ST. • LAS VEGAS, NV 89118

(702) 876-8080 • YESCO.COM

A Sign of the Times

*I*f you're looking for vintage Las Vegas, there is no better place to start than the Young Electric Sign Company (YESCO). Just take a drive down the Strip and you'll see evidence of the sixty-plus-year effect the company has had on the town and its casinos. Like the MGM marquee? They made it. New York–New York? They made that one too. Caesars Palace, Circus Circus, Wynn, TI? Yup, all of those as well. In fact, there's hardly a sign in Las Vegas that hasn't been made, maintained, or repaired by YESCO. Author Tom Wolfe once said, "Las Vegas is the only town in the world whose skyline is made up neither of buildings like New York, nor of trees . . . but signs." If that's true, then YESCO definitely had a hand in making it that way. In fact, YESCO has been in business almost as long as Vegas has been a city.

It all started with an Englishman named Thomas Young. Early in his life Thomas had an artist's eye and hand. However, there weren't a lot of opportunities for artists in Sunderland, England, in the early 1900s. So at only fifteen, Thomas dropped out of school and joined his father in the mines. Wanting more than what the local mines could offer, Thomas's father George packed up his family, put them on a boat, and headed for Montreal, Canada. From there they took a train to Ogden, Utah. That was 1910, the same year Georges Claude exhibited the first neon sign in Paris, France—an event that would eventually have a huge effect on Thomas's life.

Once in America, Thomas turned back to his artistic ways, working as a sign maker until in 1920 when he decided to go on his own. He borrowed three hundred dollars from his father and started the

Young Electric Sign Company in Ogden, Utah. In 1927 Thomas began manufacturing neon tubing. Before long he was selling neon signs in Utah, Idaho, Wyoming, and Nevada. Thomas looked for business wherever he could. "We found a 1932 phone book for the state of Nevada," says Jeff Young, Thomas's grandson. "Grandpa had checked off every business in the book." Every single business. Thomas's big break in Nevada—specifically Las Vegas, Nevada—came a year later in 1933.

In 1929 Prosper J. Goumond and A. B. Witcher opened the Boulder Club on Fremont Street in downtown Las Vegas. Two years later

Fremont Street was paved, the city's first traffic light was installed, and gambling was legalized by the Nevada state legislature. In 1933 Thomas and his wife Elmina visited the Boulder Club and Heinie Stevenson, its manager. Stevenson told Thomas he wanted to place a sign outside and asked him to design it. Thomas, who was staying at the Boulder Club, taped butcher paper to the wall of his hotel room and worked through the night rendering a sign with colored pencils. In the morning he told his wife, "Momma, if we build this sign, we're going to have to build a plant in Las Vegas."

Thomas took his design off the wall, rolled it up, and headed to Stevenson's office. When he unrolled the paper, Stevenson saw a design so amazing, so incredible that he commissioned it without even talking price. His design would prove to be the launching point for Thomas and YESCO in Las Vegas. "The Boulder Club got the ball rolling," says Jeff.

The sign Thomas designed had three parts. The top was L-shaped with the vertical word "Boulder" above the horizontal word "Club." This sign sat above a theater-style marquee that said, "Enjoy the Old West" on both sides, advertising craps, twenty-one, a bar, jackpots, and roulette underneath. At the point where the marquee's two sides met (called the bullnose) was a depiction of the Hoover Dam, which had just been constructed in nearby Boulder City. The depiction also included the dam's overflow spillways shooting out water.

While part of the sign was constructed in neon, another part used incandescent bulbs. Thomas cleverly took advantage of the heat radiated by the bulbs to make his sign do something no Las Vegas sign had ever done: have virtual motion. He placed levers behind the painted shot of the Hoover Dam. The levers, which were positioned by the spillways, had water painted on them. When the levers caught the heat generated by the bulbs, they spun. The result made the water coming from the spillways appear to be moving. All of this was done without any machine controls, meaning as long as the bulbs were on, the water was moving.

While that sign launched YESCO, it wasn't the only innovation the company made. One of its employees—Ben Jones Sr.—was an artist who also studied engineering in his spare time. At the time, most signs were constructed with cables that connected the sign to the building. The cables kept the sign in place and prevented it from falling off the building. Ben hated cables. So when he designed signs, he made sure no cables were involved. At the time, this had never been done, but it soon became the standard in the industry.

Another famous YESCO sign is the seventy-five-foot cowboy Vegas Vic, which stands under the Fremont Street Experience (which, by the way, was also created by YESCO). Vic was built in 1951 to welcome visitors to the Pioneer Club on Fremont Street. When Vic was built, he was the world's largest mechanical neon sign. Vic waved to guests for close to fifty years without interruption, which is a testament to how he was built and how he was maintained. YESCO isn't one of those companies that just builds a sign and walks away. They maintain what they build. In fact, they even maintain what other companies build. "We tend to care about all signs, no matter who built them," says Jeff.

Caring about signs is what has kept YESCO in business for ninty-four years. When it was time for Thomas to retire, he handed the reins over to his son Thomas Jr. and when Thomas Jr. retired, he again handed the business over to his sons—not sold the business to his sons. Like his father before him, he gave the business to his sons. It's something that Jeff takes very seriously. "We feel very lucky to have a place to work," Jeff says. "We're grateful to Grandpa for forging the way and making so many great contacts." Jeff says this very humbly, and you can tell his father's and grandfather's legacy has a profound influence on him. But Jeff knows his stuff, which became very apparent when he took marker in hand and began drawing the changes that had taken place in diodes (a component of LED lights) over the years on a dry-erase board.

The industry has gone from gas to incandescent lightbulbs to neon to fluorescent to translucent film to LED lights. And through it all, YESCO has remained an innovator in the industry. However, having your life revolve around signs does have a drawback. "We have this curse," Jeff explains with a smile. "We're always looking up." While most of us are looking at the building, or the scenery, or whatever catches our eye, Jeff and his crew always look at the sign, noticing a burnt-out light, or a diode that needs changing, or even admiring a sign someone else created and trying to figure out how they did it. Jeff has a good way of summing it all up: "We just love signs."

Appendix A

PLACES BY CATEGORY

Appendix B

PLACES BY NEIGHBORHOOD

Appendix C

FEATURED PLACES BY YEAR OF ORIGIN*

1860:	Spring Mountain Ranch State Park, 187
1905:	Historic Fremont Street, 97
1906:	The Golden Gate Hotel & Casino, 80
1920:	Young Electric Sign Company, 212
1933:	Boulder Dam Hotel, 19
1933:	US Post Office and Federal Courthouse (the Mob Museum), 134
1939:	MJ Christensen Diamonds, 130
1941:	El Cortez Hotel & Casino, 55
1942:	The Little Church of the West, 113
1946:	Flamingo Las Vegas (Bugsy Siegel's Monument), 24
1951:	A Little White Chapel, 117
1952:	Atomic Liquors, 1
1954:	Williams Costume Company, 208
1955:	Frankie's Tiki Room, 68
1958:	Golden Steer Steakhouse, 84
1959:	Chapel of the Flowers, 34
1959:	Freed's Bakery, 72
1960:	Tiffany's Cafe, 193
1961:	Champagnes Café, 30
1965:	Jesse's Barber Shop, 110
1965:	West Wind Las Vegas 6 Drive-in, 204
1965:	Ralph Jones Display, 210
1966:	Guardian Angel Cathedral, 89
1967:	Plant World Nursery, 169

1968: The Clark County Museum, 42

1968: The Midway at Circus Circus, 126

1970: Battista's Hole in the Wall, 10

1972: Bonanza Gift and Souvenir Shops, 14

1972: The Peppermill Restaurant and Fireside Lounge, 156

1973: Hahn's World of Surplus, 93

1975: Chicago Joe's, 38

1975: Hush Puppy Restaurant, 106

1976: Hugo's Cellar, 103

1976: Pamplemousse Le Restaurant, 152

1977: Farm Basket, 64

1977: Village Meat and Wine, 201

1978: Siena Italian Authentic Trattoria and Deli, 182

1978: Trop Aquarium, 197

1979: Doña Maria Tamales Restaurant, 51

1979: The Omelet House, 148

1980: The Auto Collection, 6

1981: Ethel M Chocolates, 60

1982: Piero's Italian Cuisine, 160

1983: Rick's Restorations, 177

1984: Di Bella Flowers and Gifts, 47

1984: Gamblers General Store, 76

1989: Lost Vegas Antiques, 122

1996: The Neon Museum, 143

2005: National Atomic Testing Museum, 138

2006: Pinball Hall of Fame, 165

2008: Retro Vegas, 173

2014: Amberjoy's Vintage Closet, 175

2014: Carlo's Bakery, 74

*Some years are approximate.

Photo Credits

All photos by the author except the following:

Page xii: Licensed by Shutterstock.com
Page 20: Courtesy of Boulder Dam Hotel
Page 36: Courtesy of Chapel of the Flowers
Page 61: Courtesy of Ethel M Chocolates
Page 98: Courtesy of Las Vegas News Bureau
Page 105: Courtesy of Hugo's Cellar
Page 114: Courtesy of Little Church of the West
Page 135: Courtesy of the Mob Museum
Page 213: Courtesy of YESCO

Index